P9-CLD-375

Vera Bradley

Cooking with Friends

our special thanks to

TOM GALLIHER ~ PHOTOGRAPHER
for picturing the food in its best light

STEPHANIE GREENLEIGH ~ FOOD STYLIST
for making the food look much better than we could

SUSAN BRITTON ~ EDITOR AND CREATIVE DIRECTOR

JOHAN ALP, JEFF BRITTON, LORI BRITTON, MEGHAN BRITTON, LESLIE BYRNE,
STEFANIE CHEVILLET, CECYLIA DACZUK, LAURA FISCHER, PEGGY GERARDOT,
KRISTI GERBER, ERIK KIM, RENEE LONG, KAREN MABEE, AND AMY RAY
for their expertise and assistance

THE PHOTOGRAPHY FOR THIS BOOK WAS TAKEN AT THE HOME AND COTTAGE
OF BARBARA BRADLEY BAEKGAARD, AND THE COTTAGE OF PATRICIA MILLER,
FOUNDERS AND CO-OWNERS OF VERA BRADLEY.

ADDITIONAL PHOTOGRAPHY AND STYLING ON PAGE 62 PROVIDED COURTESY OF
COLLEEN DUFFLEY AND MIDWEST LIVING MAGAZINE. ADDITIONAL STYLING ON COVER,
PAGES 43, 145, AND 190 PROVIDED BY BRITTON MARKETING & DESIGN GROUP

TEXT AND PHOTOGRAPHY COPYRIGHT © 2006 VERA BRADLEY

ALL RIGHTS RESERVED. NO PART OF THIS BOOK MAY BE REPRODUCED IN ANY FORM WITHOUT WRITTEN PERMISSION FROM THE PUBLISHER.

THIS COOKBOOK IS A COLLECTION OF FAVORITE RECIPES, WHICH ARE NOT NECESSARILY ORIGINAL.

LIBRARY OF CONGRESS CATALOGING-IN-PUBLICATION

DATA AVAILABLE

ISBN 1-4243-1202-7

PRINTED BY BUTLER AND TANNER LIMITED
PRINTED IN ENGLAND
SOLD THROUGHOUT THE UNITED STATES AND THROUGH VERA BRADLEY RETAILERS
TO FIND A RETAILER NEAR YOU, VISIT VERABRADLEY.COM

Come on Over!

Planning a party has its own rewards,
but when friends come tumbling in, good stories and laughter are
not far behind. It's then you realize that you don't have to entertain.
Happy people entertain themselves. It's enough to just be together,
having a good time. Of course, great food makes it even better!

Other occasions may call for careful planning, but are rewarded by
the deep, lasting memories the moment creates. Mother's china, set
amongst bouquets of bright napkins and sweet-scented florals. Tall
candles and your favorite linens, freshly pressed. Those you love most
around your table. These are the times we treasure!

In celebration of home, family and friends, we invite you to sample
some of the best recipes we have shared with each other and enjoy
"Cooking with Friends"!

Barbara Bradley Baekgaard
& Patricia Miller,
founders and
co-owners of
Vera Bradley

TABLE OF CONTENTS

Springtime

Fresh greens, petals pink, a dream whipped sky...
it's good enough to eat!

Easter Brunch

Prosecco or Moscato Spumante

Friendship Coffee Cake 12

Mandarin Orange Lettuce Salad
with Toasted Almonds 28

Shredded Parmesan Potatoes 30

Sausage Cheese Strata
with Sun-dried Tomatoes 17

Chicken en Croûte 32

Lemon Raspberry Bread Pudding 41

Mother's Day Breakfast

Orange Juice and Coffee

Soft Boiled Egg

Lemon Blueberry Bread 14

Fruit Salad with Honey-Lime Dressing 26

Mother's Day Dinner

Pinot Noir or Merlot

Warm Bleu Cheese, Bacon, and Garlic Dip
with Pita Crisps 22

Spring Greens with Strawberries and Almonds 29

Sizzling Asparagus 30

Grilled Garlic Lime Pork Tenderloin 33

Vera's Yum Yum Cake 48

Cinco de Mayo

Pink Grapefruit Margaritas 49

Black Bean Toss with Tortilla Chips 19

Guacamole and Feta Cheese with Tortilla Chips 21

Roasted Red Pepper, Corn, and Rice Salad 29

Mama's Creamy Chicken Enchiladas 35

Individual Key Lime Pies 39

Bridal Luncheon

Sparkling Raspberry Lemonade 49

Asparagus and Fontina
on Baguette with Saffron Aioli 18

Edible Flower Salad 25

Crustless Swiss Quiche 16

Orange Blossom Luncheon Cake 44

Petite Fruit Tartlets 47

Friendship Coffee Cake

The best coffee cake in the world! This delicious recipe is wonderful for Easter or any special occasion. The starter does require a little care and feeding to keep it going, but it makes enough to share with a friend every 10 days and is well worth the effort. Feed the starter on days 1 and 5. On day 10, bake the cake and share it with a friend. The next day begins day 1 again!

Starter

1 package active dry yeast
2 cups lukewarm water
1 cup flour

In a large glass bowl, dissolve the yeast in lukewarm water. (If the water is too hot it will kill the yeast.) Add flour and beat until smooth. Cover and let set at room temperature for 48 hours. Makes 2 cups of starter. Use one cup as your starter and share one cup with a special friend. (Make sure you share the recipe as well.)

Care and Feeding

1 cup flour
1 cup milk
½ cup sugar

Keep your starter in a large covered container in the refrigerator. (A gallon size plastic freezer bag actually works great and takes up less space.) On Day 1 and Day 5, feed your starter flour, milk, and sugar. On day 10 you will have 4 cups of starter. Use 2 cups for baking, 1 cup for another 10-day cycle for yourself and 1 cup for another special friend. Be sure to include the recipe.

Cake

Heat oven to 350°. Lightly grease a 9x13-inch pan. Mix the starter, sugar, eggs, and oil. Sift the dry ingredients together and blend into the starter mixture until smooth. Pour into the pan. Top the batter with the pecans and streusel topping. With the handle of a wooden spoon, poke holes into the batter so some of the topping will sink in. Bake for 45 minutes or until a toothpick inserted in the center comes out clean. Pour glaze on top. Serve warm.

Serves 10

2 cups starter

½ cup sugar

2 eggs

⅔ cup oil

2 cups flour

½ teaspoon baking powder

½ teaspoon baking soda

2 teaspoons cinnamon

½ teaspoon salt

1 cup pecans

Streusel Topping (below)

Glaze (below)

Streusel Topping

Combine butter, brown sugar, cinnamon, and flour and add to the top of the batter.

½ cup melted butter

1 cup brown sugar

2 tablespoons cinnamon

1 tablespoon flour

Glaze

Stir together the confectioner's sugar, butter, vanilla, and milk and spread on the hot coffee cake.

1 cup confectioner's sugar

1 tablespoon melted butter

½ teaspoon vanilla extract

½ teaspoon milk

Holly Lyon - Friend

Makes 1 loaf

1 ½ cups flour
1 teaspoon baking powder
⅛ teaspoon salt

6 tablespoons butter or margarine, softened
1 cup sugar

2 eggs
½ cup milk
2 teaspoons lemon zest
1 cup blueberries, tossed with
  2 teaspoons flour

Lemon Glaze (below)

⅓ cup sugar
3 tablespoons lemon juice

LEMON BLUEBERRY BREAD

This recipe was given to me by a very good friend when our family was stationed in Rome, New York. My family loves blueberries, and this is a really delicious way to have them year-round. (You can use fresh or frozen berries.)

Heat oven to 350°. Lightly grease a 5x9-inch loaf pan. Sift flour, baking powder, and salt together. In a separate bowl, cream the butter and sugar until light and fluffy. Beat in the eggs 1 at a time. Add the flour mixture alternately with the milk, beating well after each addition. (Begin and end with the flour mixture.) Fold in the lemon zest and blueberries. Pour into loaf pan.

Bake for 55 to 60 minutes or until a toothpick inserted in the center comes out clean. Pierce the warm bread with a fork. Pour the warm Lemon Glaze over the top. Cool in the pan for 30 minutes or longer. Remove to a wire rack to cool completely.

LEMON GLAZE

Combine the sugar and lemon juice in a small saucepan. Heat until the sugar dissolves, stirring frequently.

Becky Bennett - Product Development

recipe hint

Here's what to do when you check out your supply of citrus fruit, and find that it's half shriveled or you simply don't have enough. Microwave the fruit for 30 seconds and THEN squeeze! You'll get 25% more juice when the fruit has been warmed.

mother's day breakfast in bed

SUNDAY-BEST COFFEE CAKE

This is an all-time Vera Bradley favorite!

Serves 16

1 cup chopped walnuts or pecans

5 tablespoons brown sugar

1 teaspoon cinnamon

½ teaspoon pumpkin pie spice

1 cup (2 sticks) butter or margarine, softened

2 cups sugar

3 eggs

1 cup sour cream

1 teaspoon vanilla extract

2 cups flour

1 teaspoon baking powder

½ teaspoon salt

confectioners' sugar

Heat oven to 350°. Grease and flour a 10-inch tube pan. In a small bowl, mix the walnuts, brown sugar, cinnamon, and pumpkin pie spice. In a separate bowl, cream the butter, sugar, and eggs until light and fluffy. Beat in the sour cream and vanilla. Fold in the flour, baking powder, and salt.

Spoon half of the batter into the tube pan. Cover with the walnut mixture, making sure the mixture does not touch the sides of the pan. Spoon the remaining batter over the top.

Bake for 1 hour or until a toothpick inserted in the center comes out clean. Let stand until almost cool. Invert onto a serving plate. Dust with confectioners' sugar.

Joan Bradley Reedy - Daughter of Vera Bradley / South Carolina Sales Representative

CRUSTLESS SWISS QUICHES

We love these quiches—there is no crust to make.

Serves 16

½ cup (1 stick) butter or margarine

½ cup flour

1 ½ cups milk

2 ½ cups cottage cheese

1 teaspoon baking powder

1 teaspoon salt

1 teaspoon Dijon mustard

9 eggs

12 ounces cream cheese, softened

3 cups shredded Swiss cheese

⅓ cup grated Parmesan cheese

Heat oven to 350°. Grease two 10-inch pie plates. To make a white sauce, melt the butter in a medium saucepan over medium-high heat. Whisk in the flour to form a paste. Add the milk gradually, whisking constantly, and cook until thickened. Remove from heat. Cool for 15 minutes.

Combine the cottage cheese, baking powder, salt, and Dijon mustard in a bowl and mix well. In a separate bowl, beat the eggs until frothy with an electric mixer. Add the cream cheese, cottage cheese mixture, and white sauce gradually, beating constantly until well blended. Fold in the Swiss cheese and Parmesan cheese. At this point you may chill, covered, in the refrigerator until ready to bake.

Pour the batter into the prepared pie plates. Bake for 40 minutes or until puffed and light brown. Cool on a wire rack for 5 minutes. Cut into wedges and serve immediately.

Jill Nichols - Operations

SAUSAGE CHEESE STRATA WITH SUN-DRIED TOMATOES

I first served this at my son's christening. Everyone loved it so much that it has become our first choice for Sunday brunches.

Place the sun-dried tomatoes in a small, non-metal bowl. Add enough hot water to cover the tomatoes. Let stand for 15 minutes or until softened; drain.

Brown the sausage in a medium skillet over medium-high heat, stirring until crumbly. Using a slotted spoon, remove to a bowl lined with paper towels.

Grease a 9x13-inch baking dish with butter.

Whisk the milk, eggs, thyme, salt and pepper in a large bowl until blended. Add the sun-dried tomatoes, sausage, bread, onion, and Parmesan cheese and mix well. Spoon into the baking dish. Chill, covered, for 4 to 12 hours.

Preheat oven to 375°. Bake, uncovered, for 45 minutes or until puffed and golden brown. Sprinkle with the provolone cheese and goat cheese. Bake for an additional 10 minutes or until the cheese is melted. Cool on a wire rack for 5 minutes. Sprinkle with parsley and serve immediately.

Stefanie Chevillet - Friend

Serves 6 to 8

½ cup chopped sun-dried tomatoes

12 ounces hot Italian sausage, casings removed

3 ½ cups milk

8 eggs

2 teaspoons minced fresh thyme, or ¾ teaspoon dried thyme

1 ½ teaspoons salt

¼ teaspoon pepper

11 slices white bread, cut into 1-inch pieces

½ cup chopped onion

½ cup freshly grated Parmesan cheese

1 cup grated provolone cheese

¼ cup crumbled fresh goat cheese

chopped fresh parsley to taste

recipe hint

You can substitute dried herbs for fresh herbs at a ratio of one teaspoon dried to one tablespoon fresh.

Asparagus and Fontina on Baguette with Saffron Aioli

Serves 8

1 pound asparagus, trimmed

6 ounces Fontina cheese, sliced very thin

2 baguettes, sliced

Saffron Aioli (below)

This easy recipe makes an elegant presentation.

Heat oven to 350°. Steam the trimmed asparagus for 2 to 3 minutes until bright green in color. Remove from heat and plunge into a bowl of ice water and let cool. Drain and cut the asparagus into 1-inch pieces. Toast the baguettes for 6 minutes, turning off the oven halfway through.

To assemble, reheat oven to 350°. Spread 1 teaspoon of Saffron Aioli on each baguette. Top with one slice of Fontina cheese, followed by 2 pieces of asparagus. Bake until cheese is melted, about 5 minutes. Serve immediately.

Saffron Aioli

¼ cup red wine vinegar

1 tablespoon honey

large pinch of saffron threads

1 cup mayonnaise

2 garlic cloves, minced

salt and pepper to taste

Whisk the vinegar, honey, and saffron threads in a small heavy saucepan over medium-high heat. Bring to a boil. Remove from heat and cool completely. Mix mayonnaise and garlic in a medium bowl to blend. Combine with the cooled vinegar mixure. Season with salt and pepper.

Lyn Killoran - Friend

BLACK BEAN TOSS

This is a perfect accompaniment to a good margarita on a warm afternoon.

Combine the black beans, tomatoes, corn, green chilies, cilantro, and green onions in a large bowl. Add the salsa, lime juice, vinegar, oil, and Tabasco sauce and toss to mix. Chill, covered, up to 10 hours. Serve with blue corn tortilla chips.

Betsy Lewis Harned - Retailer (Betsy Anne's, Glasgow, Kentucky)

Serves 8

2 (15-ounce) cans black beans, rinsed, drained

1 (15-ounce) can diced Mexican tomatoes, drained

1 (11-ounce) can whole kernel corn, drained

1 (7-ounce) can chopped mild or hot green chilies, drained

¼ to ½ cup chopped fresh cilantro

¼ cup chopped green onions

½ cup salsa

2 tablespoons lime juice

2 tablespoons red wine vinegar

1 ½ tablespoons olive oil

⅛ teaspoon Tabasco sauce

CURRIED CHUTNEY CHEESE SPREAD

I gave this recipe to my sister and my cousin. They both brought it to the same party, and by the end of the evening they were both gone! Now, I always double the recipe. (You can freeze the extra if you don't need it all.)

Beat the cream cheese in a medium mixing bowl until smooth. Add the green onions, bacon bits, sour cream, raisins, curry powder, and nuts and mix well. Shape into a log. Chill, covered, for 6 hours or longer.

Place on a small serving platter. Pour the chutney over the top. Serve at room temperature with crackers or French bread slices.

Joanie Byrne Hall - Granddaughter of Vera Bradley / Pennsylvania Sales Representative

Serves 8

12 ounces cream cheese, softened

½ cup chopped green onions

½ cup bacon bits

2 teaspoons sour cream

½ cup raisins

½ teaspoon curry powder

½ cup chopped pecans or walnuts

1 jar Major Grey's Chutney

cinco de mayo

GUACAMOLE AND FETA CHEESE

Your guests will wonder what makes this so good. It's the feta!

Cut the avocados in half. Scoop out avocado pulp into a medium bowl. Mash with the back of a fork. Add tomatoes, onion, garlic, olive oil, lime juice, and Tabasco sauce and stir until blended. Add crumbled feta cheese to guacamole mixture. Stir and serve immediately with tortilla chips.

Kris Clifton - Friend

Serves 6

2 large ripe avocados

2 large ripe tomatoes, diced

½ red onion, diced

2 tablespoons minced garlic

2 tablespoons olive oil

1 teaspoon fresh lime juice

1 teaspoon Tabasco sauce

4 ounces crumbled feta cheese

recipe hint

Avocado flesh discolors quickly. To keep your guacamole from turning brown, add an avocado pit. You could also cover avocado dishes with lemon or lime slices, or tightly-pressed plastic wrap.

LAURA'S TACO DIP

A party favorite!

Combine the refried beans and chilies in a bowl. Spread on a large plate. Cut avocados in half and scoop out pulp into a bowl. Mash with the back of a fork and add a dash of lemon juice. Spread the avocado mixture over the refried beans.

Mix sour cream, mayonnaise, and taco seasoning in a bowl and spread over the avocados and beans. Top with black olives, tomatoes, green onions, and cheese. Serve at room temperature with tortilla chips.

Laura Byrne - Daughter-in-law of Barbara Bradley Baekgaard / Massachusetts Sales Representative

Serves 12

1 can refried beans

1 (4-ounce) can green chilies

2 avocados

dash of lemon juice

½ cup sour cream

½ cup mayonnaise

1 packet taco seasoning

¾ cup chopped black olives

¾ cup chopped tomatoes

¾ cup chopped green onions

¾ cup shredded cheddar cheese

Black Bean Toss recipe on page 19
Pink Grapefruit Margaritas recipe on page 49

Spinach and Artichoke Dip with Baked Pita Chips

Serves 8

½ cup (1 stick) butter

1 medium onion, chopped

2 packages frozen spinach, thawed and drained

1 can artichoke hearts, drained and chopped

1 (8-ounce) container sour cream

1 (8-ounce) package cream cheese, softened

1 (8-ounce) package shredded Monterey Jack cheese

8 ounces grated Parmesan cheese

Heat oven to 350°. Melt the butter in a medium skillet and add onion. Sauté onion in butter until soft, about 5 minutes.

Combine the spinach, artichoke hearts, sour cream, cream cheese, Monterey Jack cheese, and Parmesan cheese in a large bowl, stirring in the sautéed onion last. Mix well to combine. Spoon mixture into a decorative, oven-safe bowl. Bake for 20 minutes, or until bubbly and browning. Serve with tortilla chips, crackers, or pita chips.

Kris Clifton - Friend

Warm Bleu Cheese, Bacon, and Garlic Dip

Serves 8

7 slices bacon, chopped

2 garlic cloves, minced

8 ounces cream cheese, softened

¼ cup half-and-half

4 ounces crumbled bleu cheese

2 tablespoons chopped fresh chives

3 tablespoons chopped smoked almonds

Since this appetizer is always the first one to disappear, we recommend doubling the recipe.

Heat oven to 350°. Cook the bacon in a skillet until almost crisp; drain. Add the garlic, and cook for no longer than 2 minutes.

Beat the cream cheese in a mixing bowl until smooth. Add the half-and-half and blend well. Stir in the bacon mixture, bleu cheese, and chives. Spoon into an ovenproof serving dish and cover with foil.

Bake for 30 minutes or until thoroughly heated. Uncover and sprinkle with the almonds. Serve with sliced apples, toasted pita crisps, French bread baguette slices, or crackers.

Phyllis Loy - Customer Service

WHITE CHEESE MEXICAN DIP

This is so easy it can hardly be called a recipe, but every time I make it someone wants the "recipe."

Combine the sour cream, cottage cheese, pepper-jack cheese, and green onions in a bowl and mix well. Add the jalapeño chile and mix well. Serve with tortilla chips or corn chips.

Amy Byrne Ray - Granddaughter of Vera Bradley

Serves 8

2 cups sour cream

16 ounces cottage cheese

8 ounces grated pepper-jack cheese

1 bunch green onions, sliced

½ jalapeño chile, minced, or Tabasco sauce to taste

CHICKEN AND CORN TOSTADA SALAD

Great summer dish—well worth trying for your family.

Heat the oil in a large skillet over medium-high heat. Add the chicken. Cook for 5 to 7 minutes, or until cooked through. Remove to a large bowl and sprinkle with the garlic salt. Stir in the corn. Chill, covered, for 30 minutes. Add the tomatoes, beans, green onions, and avocados and toss to mix well.

Combine the vinegar, honey, cumin, salt and pepper in a jar with a tight-fitting lid. Cover and shake well. Pour over the chicken mixture and toss to coat well.

To serve, arrange the lettuce and bell pepper on each serving plate. Add the chicken mixture. Top with the cheese and tortilla chips. Garnish with salsa and sour cream.

Dan's Tog Shop - Retailer, Menomonee Falls, Wisconsin

Serves 4

1 tablespoon olive oil

2 boneless skinless chicken breasts, cut into strips

½ teaspoon garlic salt

1 (16-ounce) can whole kernel corn, drained

1 cup chopped tomatoes

1 (15-ounce) can black beans, drained, rinsed

5 green onions with tops, thinly sliced

2 medium avocados, peeled, chopped

¼ cup cider vinegar

3 tablespoons honey

1½ teaspoons cumin

¼ teaspoon salt

¼ teaspoon pepper

1 head Boston or Bibb lettuce, torn into bite-size pieces

1 small red bell pepper, chopped

2 cups shredded Monterey Jack cheese

3 cups lightly crushed blue corn tortilla chips

edible flower salad

Curried Chicken Salad

Prepare grill. Place the chicken on a grill rack. Grill over hot coals until cooked through. Let stand until cool. Cut into bite-size pieces.

Combine the chicken, grapes, celery, almonds, and parsley in a large bowl. Add the Curried Mayonnaise and stir until moistened. Serve on lettuce-lined serving plates.

Note: This salad also makes a delicious sandwich served on a croissant.

Serves 4

4 chicken breasts
1 cup green grape halves
¼ cup chopped celery
½ cup toasted almonds
½ cup minced parsley
Curried Mayonnaise (below)

Curried Mayonnaise

Blend the mayonnaise, milk, curry powder, ginger, salt and white pepper in a bowl. Adjust the seasonings to taste.

Vicki Kim - Friend

1 cup mayonnaise
⅓ cup milk
1 tablespoon curry powder
2 teaspoons ginger
salt and white pepper to taste

Edible Flower Salad

Combine the greens and fresh herbs; toss with Raspberry Vinaigrette. Sprinkle the salad with the edible flowers.

Serves 4

4 cups spring greens
½ cup chopped fresh basil
½ cup chopped fresh parsley
¼ cup chopped fresh chives
assorted fresh edible flowers
  (nasturtium, pansy, rose)
Raspberry Vinaigrette (below)

Raspberry Vinaigrette

In a small bowl, whisk together all the ingredients. Let stand 10 minutes.

Anne Frantz - Merchandising

¼ cup olive oil
2 teaspoons Dijon mustard
1 tablespoon raspberry vinegar
2 teaspoons sugar
1 teaspoon garlic salt
1 teaspoon chopped fresh basil
⅛ teaspoon salt
pepper to taste

Fruit Salad
with Honey-Lime Dressing

Serves 4

2 cups diced, peeled cantaloupe

2 cups diced, peeled honeydew melon

2 cups seedless red or green grapes

2 cups diced, peeled, cored pineapple

1 ½ cups diced, peeled papaya

1 cup halved, hulled strawberries

Honey-Lime Dressing (below)

This dish is not too difficult, yet makes a nice presentation for company.

Combine cantaloupe, honeydew, grapes, pineapple, papaya, and strawberries in a large bowl. Chill, covered, in the refrigerator for up to 6 hours. When ready to serve, mix with chilled Honey-Lime Dressing. Let the fruit salad stand for 15 minutes to blend the flavors.

Honey-Lime Dressing

½ cup plain yogurt

¼ cup fresh lime juice

¼ cup honey

1 teaspoon lime zest

Whisk the yogurt, lime juice, honey, and lime zest in a small bowl to blend. Chill, covered, in the refrigerator until ready to serve.

Cheri Lantz - Sales

recipe hint

Measuring honey, syrups and molasses can be a messy job. Try lightly coating the measuring cup with a small amount of oil before adding the sticky stuff. After measuring, the contents will slide out and your careful measurements will be more accurate, since less will be left in the cup.

Sarah Schneider (pictured right), friend of Vera Bradley

garden bridal luncheon

Serves 6 to 8

6 slices bacon

2 large heads Bibb or Boston lettuce

1 (8-ounce) can mandarin oranges, drained

¼ cup toasted almonds

Vinaigrette (below)

1 cup salad oil

¼ cup vinegar

2 teaspoons salt

1 teaspoon paprika

1 teaspoon pepper

¼ teaspoon dry mustard

¼ teaspoon confectioners' sugar

Mandarin Orange and Lettuce Salad

Easy and pretty!

Cook the bacon in a skillet until crisp. Remove to paper towels to drain. Crumble the bacon.

Tear the lettuce into bite-size pieces into a large salad bowl. Add the oranges, almonds, and bacon. Toss with enough Vinaigrette to coat. You may add sliced celery and green onions if desired.

Vinaigrette

Combine the oil, vinegar, salt, paprika, pepper, dry mustard, and confectioners' sugar in a container with a tight-fitting lid. Cover and shake well. Chill until ready to use. You may store in the refrigerator for several weeks.

Sharon Keogh - Retailer (Monograms & More, Hinsdale, Illinois)

ROASTED RED PEPPER, CORN, AND RICE SALAD

An excellent summer salad—sure to be made often. It tastes best made with fresh sweet corn.

Melt the margarine in a medium saucepan over medium-high heat. Add the rice. Sauté until almost brown. Add the water and salt. Cook for 20 minutes or until just tender, stirring until all of the liquid has been absorbed. Spoon into a large bowl. Cool to room temperature. You may chill, covered, in the refrigerator to speed up the chilling process.

Whisk the mayonnaise in a small bowl until smooth. Add the buttermilk, Parmesan cheese, and vinegar and whisk to blend well.

Combine the rice, corn, roasted peppers, and ½ cup of the green onions in a large serving bowl and mix well. Stir in the mayonnaise mixture and season with salt and pepper. Sprinkle with the remaining ¼ cup of green onions. Serve at room temperature.

Kathy Reedy Ray - Granddaughter of Vera Bradley / Michigan Sales Representative

Serves 6 to 8

1 tablespoon margarine
1 ½ cups long grain white rice
3 cups water
2 teaspoons salt

¼ cup mayonnaise
½ cup buttermilk
⅓ cup grated Parmesan cheese
1 tablespoon red wine vinegar

2 cups fresh whole kernel corn or thawed and drained frozen whole kernel corn
1 (14-ounce) jar roasted red peppers, cut into ½-inch pieces
¾ cup thinly sliced green onions
salt and pepper to taste

recipe hint

Always stir rice with a fork… in fact, use two forks. Using a spoon bruises the grains and makes the rice sticky.

SPRING GREENS WITH STRAWBERRIES AND ALMONDS

This is a nice spring salad when strawberries are at their best.

Divide the spring greens among 4 salad plates. Arrange the strawberries and bleu cheese on each salad. Sprinkle with almonds. Drizzle with the salad dressing. Serve immediately. You may sprinkle with garlic and herb croutons for an added crunch.

Patti Reedy Parker - Granddaughter of Vera Bradley / North & South Carolina Sales Representative

Serves 4

6 cups spring greens
1 cup sliced fresh strawberries
¼ cup crumbled bleu cheese
½ cup slivered almonds
¾ cup poppy seed salad dressing
garlic and herb croutons (optional)

Shredded Parmesan Potatoes

Serves 8

8 medium potatoes

2 bunches green onions with tops, sliced
½ cup grated Parmesan cheese
2 teaspoons salt
2 teaspoons pepper
¼ cup (½ stick) butter, cut into pats
paprika to taste

Heat oven to 350°. Prepare a 9x13-inch baking dish by spraying with nonstick cooking spray. Place the potatoes in a large stockpot with enough water to cover. Boil for 20 minutes or until tender; drain. Cool slightly. Peel the potatoes. Shred with a knife or in a food processor.

Place in a large mixing bowl. Add the green onions. Stir in the Parmesan cheese, salt and pepper. Spoon into the baking dish. Dot with butter. Sprinkle with paprika.

Bake for 40 minutes or until the top begins to brown. Let stand for 10 minutes before serving.

Patricia Miller - Founder and Co-owner

Sizzling Asparagus

Serves 2 to 4

1 pound fresh asparagus, trimmed
1½ tablespoons olive oil
   (preferably extra-virgin)
1 tablespoon kosher salt

1 tablespoon basalmic vinegar (optional)

Heat oven to 450°. Place asparagus in a large shallow baking pan. Drizzle with oil and sprinkle with salt. Roast in oven for 3 minutes. Shake pan and roast until the asparagus is bright green, about 1 to 2 minutes longer. Serve with a sprinkling of vinegar if desired.

Stefanie Chevillet - Friend

recipe hint

Olive oil designations are made based on processing methods as well as flavor. Virgin oils contain no refined oil. "Extra-virgin" is given to oil from the first pressing. Oil noted simply as "olive oil" is a blend, containing refined oil, which alters the flavor.

*Pictured above right:
Sarah Schneider, Holly Wagner, Alicia Wilkins, and Megan Kjesbo;
friends and associates of Vera Bradley*

CHICKEN EN CROÛTE

Serves 6

8 ounces mushrooms

3 shallots

salt and pepper to taste

6 boneless chicken breasts, diced

4 tablespoons butter

1 (10-ounce) can cream of chicken soup

1 (17-ounce) package frozen puff pastry (thawed)

egg whites, lightly beaten

I had this dish at a friend's house and LOVED it. I then served it at a wedding shower, everyone raved. It is both delicious and beautiful to serve.

Heat oven to 400°. Chop or grind mushrooms and shallots. Place in skillet; cook on low heat until moisture evaporates. Season with salt and pepper. In a skillet, sear diced chicken in hot melted butter and let cool. Add the soup to the chicken.

Unfold pastry on a lightly floured surface; cut into large squares. Spoon a heaping tablespoon of chicken and soup mixture in the middle of each square. Spoon a teaspoon of mushroom mixture on top. Bring the points of the pastry together at the top and ruffle all the edges that meet to seal the pastry together. Arrange on a nonstick baking sheet. Brush with egg whites and pierce with a fork.

Bake for 20 minutes or until cooked through and golden brown.

Note: May be assembled a day ahead. Chill wrapped chicken puffs in a refrigerator. Take out and bring to room temperature before baking.

Glenna Reno - Michigan Sales Representative

entertaining hint

For an easy to manage event:
- Set the table early in the day and plan all serving utensils and dishes.
- Make recipes that can be made the day before so only one or two items need to be cooked just before your guests arrive. We've included many recipes that will cater to early preparation.
- Set desserts on the side so they add to the decor and tempt the palette during the meal.

Grilled Garlic Lime Pork Tenderloin

A great entrée to serve for a dinner party. The presentation is beautiful and it is very easy to make.

Process the garlic, soy sauce, ginger root, Dijon mustard, lime juice, oil, cayenne pepper, salt and pepper in a blender or food processor until blended. Place the pork in a large plastic food storage bag. Pour the marinade over the pork and seal the bag. Place in a shallow dish. Marinate in the refrigerator for 24 hours, turning occasionally.

Prepare grill. Let pork stand at room temperature for 30 minutes before grilling. Drain the pork, discarding the marinade. Place on an oiled grill rack. Grill 5 to 6 inches above glowing coals for 15 to 20 minutes or until cooked through, turning every 5 minutes. Remove the pork to a cutting board. Let stand for 5 minutes. Cut into slices. Serve with Onion Jalapeño Marmalade.

Onion Jalapeño Marmalade

Sauté the onions in the oil in a large heavy saucepan over medium heat until softened. Add the chiles. Sauté for 1 minute. Add the honey. Cook for 1 minute. Add the vinegar. Simmer until almost all of the liquid is evaporated, stirring constantly. Add the water. Simmer for 10 minutes or until slightly thickened, stirring constantly. Season with salt and pepper.

You may prepare up to 2 days ahead, and store, covered, in the refrigerator. Reheat before serving.

Lyn Killoran - Friend

Serves 6

6 large garlic cloves, chopped

2 tablespoons soy sauce

2 tablespoons grated fresh ginger root

2 teaspoons Dijon mustard

⅓ cup fresh lime juice

½ cup olive oil

cayenne pepper to taste

salt and pepper to taste

4 (¾-pound) pork tenderloins

Onion Jalapeño Marmalade (below)

1 ¼ pounds red or yellow onions, thinly sliced, separated into rings

3 tablespoons olive oil

2 fresh jalapeño chiles, seeded, minced

2 tablespoons honey or sugar

3 to 4 tablespoons red wine vinegar

¼ cup water

salt and pepper to taste

recipe hint

Capsaicin—the chemical that gives chile peppers their burn—is dangerous to skin and eyes, so handle them with gloves or oiled hands. Don't cut on wooden surfaces or under running water, and process at arm's length. Counteract the burning with a bit of sugar or a sip of a dairy product.

HOT CHICKEN SALAD

Serves 4 to 6

2 cups cooked, diced chicken

1 ½ cups celery

¼ cup toasted almonds

2 teaspoons minced onion

½ cup mayonnaise

1 tablespoon lemon juice

salt and pepper to taste

1 cup shredded cheddar cheese

1 tablespoon toasted almonds
 or breadcrumbs

Great for showers and luncheons!

Heat oven to 350°. Mix chicken, celery, almonds, and onion. Add mayonnaise, lemon juice, salt and pepper. Place in a casserole dish. Top with cheese and almonds or bread crumbs. Bake for 25 to 30 minutes, or until heated through and lightly browned.

Holly Wagner - Customer Service

LILA'S CHICKEN

Serves 8

8 ounces vermicelli

½ cup (1 stick) butter

1 large onion, chopped

1 ½ cups sliced fresh mushrooms

1 (10-ounce) can cream of chicken soup

1 (10-ounce) can cream of mushroom soup

2 cups chicken broth

4 boneless skinless chicken breasts, cut
 into bite-size pieces

2 cups sour cream

seasoned pepper to taste

1 cup shredded cheddar cheese

½ cup grated Parmesan cheese

½ cup shredded cheddar cheese

5 slices rye bread, cut into cubes

If you've ever been to the Baekgaards' for dinner, chances are you've had this!

Heat oven to 350°. Grease a 8x12-inch baking dish. Boil the vermicelli for 2 minutes; drain.

Melt the butter in a large skillet. Add the onion. Sauté until translucent. Combine the sautéed onion, mushrooms, soups, chicken broth, and uncooked chicken in a large bowl and mix well. Add the sour cream, seasoned pepper, and cheddar cheese. Stir in the slightly cooked pasta.

Spoon into the baking dish. Sprinkle with the Parmesan cheese and cheddar cheese. Sprinkle the bread cubes over the top. Bake for 1 hour or until the chicken is cooked through.

Barbara Bradley Baekgaard - Founder and Co-owner

Mama's Creamy Chicken Enchiladas

As a working mother, time is of the essence. This recipe is easy, fast, and delicious when there is not much time for cooking.

Heat oven to 350°. Spray a 9x13-inch baking pan with nonstick cooking spray.

To make the chicken filling, melt the butter in a large skillet. Add the chilies, onion, and garlic. Sauté until tender, about 4 minutes. Add salt and pepper and sauté 1 minute longer. Stir in chicken strips and cream cheese and cook until all of the cheese has melted. Remove from heat.

Fill each tortilla with chicken mixture and roll up. Place seam side down in the pan. Cover enchiladas with shredded cheese. Enchiladas can be made to this point one day in advance and chilled, covered, in the refrigerator.

Drizzle half-and-half over cheese-covered enchiladas. Bake for 45 minutes. Serve with shredded lettuce, salsa, guacamole, and chips.

Kate Miller - Customer Service

Serves 6

1 tablespoon butter
2 (4-ounce) cans chilies, drained
1 medium yellow onion, chopped
1 tablespoon minced garlic
salt and pepper to taste
4 cups precooked seasoned chicken strips
1 (8-ounce) package cream cheese

6 large flour tortillas
3 cups shredded Monterey Jack cheese
½ pint half-and-half

Serves 10 to 12

1 (10- to 12-pound) bone-in smoked ham

When selecting a ham, choose one with a substantial layer of exterior fat. Use only half of the spice rub if the fat layer is less than ⅛-inch thick.

2 cups sparkling apple cider

½ cup dry sherry

2 tablespoons coriander seeds

1½ tablespoons cumin seeds

1 tablespoon fennel seeds

2 teaspoons cardamom pods, seeds only

1 tablespoon light brown sugar

1 teaspoon salt

¼ teaspoon cayenne pepper

1 cup water

Mango-Cranberry Chutney (below)

Makes 4½ cups

1 teaspoon peanut oil

1 small sweet onion, chopped

pinch of salt

1 teaspoon curry powder

1 cinnamon stick, broken in half

1 cup granulated sugar

1 cup light brown sugar

½ cup cider vinegar

2 large under-ripe mangoes, peeled and cut into ¾-inch cubes

1 pound frozen cranberries

2 teaspoons peanut oil

1 teaspoon mustard seeds

SPICED SMOKED HAM

Spicy, smoky, sweet. This ham makes a presentation fit for a king. (Trumpet fanfare optional.)

Heat oven to 350°. Remove the rind from the ham and trim the fat to a ½ inch layer. Using a sharp knife, score the fat in a crosshatch pattern without cutting into the meat.

Set the ham in a large roasting pan, fat side up; add the cider and sherry and cover loosely with foil. Bake for 4 hours, basting with the pan juices every half hour, adding water if the pan looks dry. The ham is done when golden brown and thermometer registers 150°. Transfer to another roasting pan.

In a medium skillet, toast the coriander, cumin, fennel, and cardamom seeds over moderate heat until fragrant, about 2 minutes. Transfer to a spice grinder and let cool completely, then coarsely grind. Mix in the sugar, salt, and cayenne. Sprinkle the spice mixture over the ham, lightly pressing it into the crosshatched fat. Bake the ham for an additional 20 minutes. Remove from the roasting pan and let it stand for 15 minutes before cutting.

Set the roasting pan on the stovetop over high heat until sizzling. Add water and simmer, scraping up the browned bits, until reduced to ¼ cup. Pour the pan juices into a bowl and skim off the fat. Carve the ham into thin slices and arrange on a platter. Serve with the pan juices and Mango-Cranberry Chutney.

MANGO-CRANBERRY CHUTNEY

In a large saucepan, heat the peanut oil. Add the onion and salt and cook over moderately low heat, stirring until the onion softens, about 8 minutes. Add the curry and cinnamon stick and cook for 1 minute. Stir in the sugars and vinegar and bring to a boil. Add the mangoes and cook, stirring occasionally, until softened, about 35 to 40 minutes. Add the cranberries and cook over moderate heat for 40 minutes, crushing them against the sides of the pan.

In a separate saucepan, heat the peanut oil. Add the mustard seeds and cook until they begin to pop. Immediately stir in the chutney. Transfer to a bowl and let cool.

Note: Make ahead. The chutney can be refrigerated for up to 2 weeks.

Debra Bleeke - Customer Service

Molly Ray, Caroline Ray, Alexandra Yoder, Ellen Chevillet, Allison Gray, Olivia Ray, Meredith Gray and Annie Chevillet

Caramel Chocolate Squares

When I have a request for brownies, I always make this recipe and no one is ever disappointed. They are fabulous.

Makes 3 dozen

1 (14-ounce) package caramels (about 50)
⅓ cup evaporated milk

1 (2-layer) package German chocolate cake mix
¾ cup (1 ½ sticks) butter, melted
⅓ cup evaporated milk

2 cups chocolate chips
1 cup chopped pecans (optional)

Heat oven to 350°. Butter and flour a 9x13-inch baking pan. Melt the caramels with evaporated milk in a saucepan over low heat, stirring constantly. Remove from heat.

Combine the cake mix, butter, and evaporated milk in a medium bowl. Mix with a wooden spoon until the dough holds together. Press half of the dough in the bottom of the baking pan.

Bake for 6 minutes. Remove from the oven. Sprinkle with the chocolate chips and pecans. Pour the caramel mixture evenly over the chocolate layer. Crumble the remaining dough over the top. Bake for 18 minutes. Refrigerate immediately after baking and chill for 30 minutes. Cut into squares.

Julie Clymer - Distribution

INDIVIDUAL KEY LIME PIES

These little pies can be made days in advance and last for up to a month (tightly wrapped) in the freezer—just decorate them with lime slices right before serving. They are very cute and everyone loves them.

Heat oven to 350°. Line a cupcake muffin tin with paper liners. For the crust, combine the graham cracker crumbs, sugar, and butter in the bowl of a food processor. Process until combined. Press 1 tablespoon of the crumb mixture into each liner, making sure that the sides and bottom are of an even thickness. Bake for 5 to 7 minutes. Allow to cool completely.

For the filling, beat the egg yolks and sugar on high speed in the bowl of an electric mixer fitted with a paddle attachment for 5 minutes, until thick. With the mixer on medium speed, add the condensed milk, lime zest, and lime juice and mix well until smooth. Pour filling into the individual cups and freeze for several hours or overnight.

When ready to serve, beat the heavy cream on high speed until soft peaks form. Add the sugar and vanilla and beat until firm. Pipe the whipped cream decoratively around the edges of each pie. Slice the key limes about ¼ inch thick and twist. Place 1 slice in the middle of each individual pie.

Stephanie Scheele - Marketing

Makes 2 dozen

1 ½ cups graham cracker crumbs (1 sleeve of graham crackers)

¼ cup sugar

6 tablespoons butter, melted

8 extra large egg yolks, room temperature

⅓ cup sugar

1 (14-ounce) can sweetened condensed milk

2 tablespoons lime zest

1 cup key lime juice (available in the international and juice aisles)

1 cup cold heavy whipping cream

¼ cup sugar

¼ teaspoon vanilla extract

6 key limes

recipe hint

Key limes are smaller and more flavorful than the common lime, also known as a Persian lime. Don't confuse the two.

LEMON RASPBERRY
BREAD PUDDING

A lovely springtime variation of a classic favorite.

Heat oven to 350°. To make bread pudding: Evenly spread the raspberries on the bottom of a 9x13-inch pan. Place the bread pieces on top of the raspberries.

Warm the milk, cream, sugar, salt, and lemon zest in a medium saucepan over medium heat, stirring frequently, until the liquid is very hot and the sugar has dissolved, about 5 minutes.

To make the custard: Whisk together the eggs and egg yolks in a large bowl. Whisk the hot cream mixture, a little at a time, into the eggs.

Pour the custard into the pan over the raspberries and bread pieces. Using a spatula, press the bread pieces into the custard, coating them well. Bake the custard for 40 minutes.

While the custard is baking, combine the cinnamon and sugar in a small bowl. Sprinkle the cinnamon sugar over the top of the bread pudding and continue baking about 10 minutes longer or until the tips of the bread pieces are golden brown and a small knife inserted in the middle is coated with thickened custard.

Let cool at least 15 minutes before serving. Serve the bread pudding warm.

Note: The custard can be made a day or two in advance; refrigerate until ready to make the bread pudding. The bread pudding can be baked a day in advance. Keep refrigerated and reheat in a 300° oven for about 20 minutes. Delicious with fresh raspberries.

Pat Neulle - Friend

Serves 8

1 pint raspberries

1 baguette, crust on, cut into ¾-inch pieces (about 4 ½ cups)

2 ¼ cups milk

2 ¼ cups heavy whipping cream

⅔ cup sugar

¼ teaspoon salt

zest of 3 lemons

3 large eggs

3 large egg yolks

¼ teaspoon cinnamon

1 ½ tablespoons sugar

Pictured: Allison Gray, friend of Vera Bradley, with Molly Ray, great-granddaughter of Vera Bradley

LEMON SWIRL CHEESECAKE

Serves 12

6 whole graham crackers (about 3 ounces)

1 cup toasted walnuts

3 tablespoons melted butter

2 teaspoons lemon zest

16 ounces cream cheese, softened

½ cup sugar

½ cup frozen lemonade concentrate, thawed

2 teaspoons lemon zest

¾ cup sour cream

2 eggs

1 cup sour cream, at room temperature

1 (11-ounce) jar lemon curd

⅔ cup chilled whipping cream

2 (¼-inch) lemon slices, cut into 4 wedges each

8 small sprigs of mint

This is an elegant dessert for true lemon lovers.

Heat oven to 350°. Process the graham crackers in a food processor until finely ground. Add the walnuts. Process until coarsely chopped. Add the butter and lemon zest. Process just until moistened. Press over the bottom of a 9-inch springform pan. Bake for 10 minutes or until set. Cool on a wire rack.

Beat the cream cheese, sugar, lemonade concentrate, and lemon zest in a large mixing bowl until smooth. Beat in sour cream. Add the eggs 1 at a time, beating just until combined. Pour into the crust. Bake for 50 minutes or until the center moves slightly when the pan is shaken. Cool for 5 minutes on a wire rack.

Whisk sour cream in a small bowl until smooth. Whisk the lemon curd in a small bowl until smooth. Run a sharp knife around the side of the cheesecake. Alternate small dollops of sour cream and lemon curd side by side in concentric circles atop the warm cheesecake, covering the top completely and starting at the outside edge. Shake the pan gently to smooth out the toppings. Swirl the topping gently with the tip of a knife to marbleize. Chill, covered, for 8 to 12 hours.

Beat the whipping cream in a medium bowl until soft peaks form. Spoon into a pastry bag fitted with a medium star tip. Run a sharp knife around the side of the cheesecake to loosen. Release the side of the pan. Place the cheesecake on a cake platter. Pipe the whipped cream in a decorative scalloped border around the top edge. Garnish with lemon wedges and mint sprigs.

Leslie Byrne - Daughter-in-law of Barbara Bradley Baekgaard

lemon swirl cheesecake

Serves 12 to 16

1 ½ cups flour, sifted

1 ½ teaspoons baking powder

¼ teaspoon salt

1 cup (2 sticks) butter or margarine,
 softened

1 cup sugar

1 tablespoon orange zest

2 eggs

½ cup orange juice

1 tablespoon orange liqueur

1 teaspoon lemon juice

½ teaspoon vanilla extract

Candied Orange Peel (below)

1 large orange

3 tablespoons light corn syrup

¼ cup sugar

ORANGE BLOSSOM LUNCHEON CAKE

This is a beautiful cake to serve at any luncheon.

Heat oven to 350°. Grease and flour a 6-cup bundt pan. Whisk the flour, baking powder, and salt in a bowl. In a separate bowl, beat the butter at medium speed until creamy, scraping the bowl occasionally. Add sugar gradually, beating constantly for 5 to 7 minutes or until light and fluffy. Add the orange zest, then the eggs 1 at a time, beating just until blended.

Add the flour mixture alternately with the orange juice to the butter mixture, beating constantly at low speed until blended after each addition and beginning and ending with the flour mixture. Stir in the liqueur, lemon juice, and vanilla. Spoon the batter into the bundt pan.

Bake for 35 to 40 minutes or until a wooden pick inserted in the center comes out clean. Cool in the pan on a wire rack for 10 minutes. Invert onto the wire rack to cool completely. Sprinkle Candied Orange Peel over the cooled cake.

CANDIED ORANGE PEEL

Peel the orange and cut the peel into ⅛-inch strips. Reserve the orange sections for another use. Combine the peel and corn syrup in a saucepan. Bring to a boil over medium heat; reduce heat. Cook for 3 to 4 minutes, stirring frequently.

Combine the peel with sugar in a bowl and toss to coat. Spread in a single layer on waxed paper. Let stand until dry.

Patricia Miller - Founder and Co-owner

orange blossom luncheon cake

petite fruit tartlets

Petite Fruit Tartlets

These are quick and easy for unexpected guests. You can make them in 10 minutes, as long as you have the tart shells in the freezer. They allow you to be creative, because you can fill them with almost anything.

Makes 12 tartlets

12 prepared frozen mini tart shells
strawberry, raspberry, or apricot jam
fresh berries and fruit
whipped cream

Heat oven to 350°. Place ½ teaspoon of jam in each tart shell. Bake for 5 to 10 minutes. The shells are precooked so they don't need much time. When jam starts to bubble, remove and let cool. Top with 3 or 4 berries and whipped cream just before serving. Add a berry on top for garnish.

Here are some additional variations:

LEMON TARTLETS: Fill cooled, baked shells with lemon curd and top with whipped cream. Garnish with a raspberry and mint sprig.

CHOCOLATE TARTLETS: Fill cooled, baked shells with chocolate mousse or pudding. Top with whipped cream and chocolate shavings or nonpareils.

BRIE CHEESE APPETIZER: Place a small slice of Brie cheese in the bottom of each shell before baking. Bake for 5 minutes or until cheese is melted. Top with chutney or Hot Pepper Jelly (page 160). Garnish with a pecan half.

Anne Frantz - Merchandising

VERA'S YUM YUM CAKE

Serves 15

1 (2-layer) package yellow cake mix

8 ounces cream cheese, softened

1 (4-ounce) package vanilla instant
    pudding mix

1 cup milk

16 ounces whipped topping

2 (16-ounce) packages fresh strawberries or
    frozen strawberries, thawed

2 cups shredded coconut

1 cup chopped walnuts

A slice of cake is always a treat. My mother always had a cake in the kitchen when we were growing up. She served this one for all of her grandchildren's birthdays. They still love it to this day.

Prepare and bake the cake using the package directions for a 9x13-inch cake pan. Cool in the pan on a wire rack.

Beat the cream cheese in a mixing bowl until light and fluffy. Add the pudding mix and milk and beat until smooth. Fold in the whipped topping. Spread over the cooled cake. Arrange the strawberries evenly over the cake. Sprinkle with the coconut and walnuts. Chill, covered, for 4 to 6 hours before serving.

Barbara Bradley Baekgaard - Founder and Co-owner

PINK GRAPEFRUIT MARGARITAS

This fruity, tangy treat can turn your next party into a real fiesta! Cha-cha-cha! (Pictured on page 20.)

Mix the grapefruit juice, lime juice, tequila, Grand Marnier, and sugar in a pitcher. Fill a blender container with crushed ice. Add ⅓ of the juice mixture. Process at high speed until frothy. Pour into 3 or 4 chilled salt- or sugar-rimmed glasses. Repeat 2 more times. Garnish each serving with a slice of lime and a sprig of mint.

Jill Nichols - Operations

Serves 9 to 12

4 cups fresh pink grapefruit juice
juice of 3 limes
2 cups tequila
¼ cup Grand Marnier
1 cup sugar

SPARKLING RASPBERRY LEMONADE

A perfectly pretty party punch! (Pictured on page 50.)

Combine the raspberries, sugar, and water in a medium saucepan. Cook over medium heat until the sugar dissolves, stirring constantly. Increase heat to high and bring to a boil. Boil for 3 to 4 minutes. Strain into a bowl, discarding the seeds and solids. Add the lemon zest and mix well. Chill, covered, in the refrigerator until ready to serve.

Combine the raspberry syrup mixture, lemon juice, and club soda in a large pitcher and blend well. Serve over ice in glasses. Garnish the drink with fresh raspberries and place a slice of lemon on the edge of each glass.

Stacie Gray - Friend

Serves 6

1 (12-ounce) package frozen unsweetened raspberries, or 3 cups fresh
1 cup sugar
½ cup water

1 ½ tablespoons lemon zest

1 cup fresh lemon juice
1 (1-liter) bottle club soda

sparkling raspberry lemonade

Summer Coconut Mojito

Get your mojo going with this mojito.

Muddle mint, lime juice, and sugar in a shaker. Shake vigorously. Add ice and Bacardi Coco. Shake and strain into a martini glass rimmed with coconut.

Melissa Cordial - Marketing

Serves 1

3 sprigs fresh mint
1 ounce fresh lime juice
1 teaspoon sugar
3 ounces Bacardi Coco
shredded coconut

Sunny Sangria

A refreshing and light drink, perfect for a spring or summer party on the beach or the deck.

Place the orange and lemon in a large punch bowl. Sprinkle with the confectioners' sugar. Mash the fruit lightly. Stir in the grape juice and cranberry juice cocktail. Chill until serving time. Add the wine and club soda just before serving. You may serve over ice.

Julie North - Human Resources

Serves 10 to 12

1 orange, thinly sliced
1 lemon, thinly sliced
2 tablespoons confectioners' sugar
1 cup grape juice
4 cups cranberry juice cocktail

2 bottles dry red wine
2 cups club soda

Sparkling Raspberry Lemonade recipe on page 49.

Summer

Summertime in Indiana is a wonderful mix of baseball,
blue skies, late evening cook-outs, and relaxing lakeside.

Fourth of July

LEMONADE

SUMMERTIME SALSA WITH TORTILLA CHIPS 67

CHOP HOUSE COLESLAW 68

CORN SALAD 71

WHISKEY BARBEQUE RIBS 84

BERRY CREAM PIE 87

GIANT CHOCOLATE CHIP COOKIES
SANDWICHED WITH VANILLA ICE CREAM 88

Seaside Dinner

CHILLED WHITE WINE

CHILLED CORN & BUTTERMILK BISQUE WITH CRAB 58

SAVORY CHEESE BISCUITS 65

WARM SWISS CHEESE AND BACON DIP
WITH CRACKERS 67

ROASTED BELL PEPPER PASTA 77

ANNAPOLIS CRAB CAKES 78

SUMMER SHRIMP BOIL 84

HILLSBORO CLUB BLUEBERRY COOKIES 90

Summer Evening Party on the Porch

Assorted Beverages and Beer

Fruit Salsa with Cinnamon Crisps 63

Potato Pizza 64

Salsa-Baked Goat Cheese with
Toasted Pita Chips 65

Potato Salad with Bleu Cheese and Bacon 72

Fillet of Beef with Gorgonzola Sauce 81

Indiana Mint Brownies 91

Lemon Cake with Whiskey Glaze 93

Ruth's Italian Pound Cake 95

Family Reunion

Rhubarb Slush 97

Baked Southwestern Corn Dip
with Tortilla Chips 60

Beer Cheese Dip with Crackers 60

French Bread with Pesto Spread 61

Creole Potato Salad 71

Eight-Vegetable Marinated Salad 72

Chip's Grilled Potatoes 75

Flank Steak with Marinade 81

Grilled Chicken 83

Georgia Chess Pie 87

Happy Oatmeal Cookies 88

Nectarine Coconut Cake 94

Blueberry Pecan French Toast

Truly the best French toast you've ever tasted. No syrup necessary.

Put bread cubes in a large, non-metal bowl. Whip eggs, sugar, cinnamon, and nutmeg until light in color, thick, and airy, approximately 10 minutes. Add milk, vanilla, and dash of salt. Stir, and pour over bread. Cover and refrigerate overnight.

In the morning, preheat oven to 325°. Lightly grease a 9x13-inch baking pan. Mix 1 cup blueberries into egg and bread mixture and pour into the baking pan. Sprinkle remaining blueberries on top, followed by the pecans.

In a separate heavy saucepan over medium heat, combine the butter and brown sugar. Cook until mixture is thick and comes to a low boil. Pour over blueberries and pecans.

Bake on the center rack for approximately 1 hour or until puffed. Let rest 15 minutes before serving.

Note: This dish is very good served at room temperature or cold from the refrigerator, with a dollop of whipped cream.

Lori Britton - Friend

Serves 6 to 8

8 cups French bread cut into 1-inch cubes (this should be 1 large loaf, but 2 would be safe)

5 eggs

1 cup sugar

1 teaspoon cinnamon

1 teaspoon nutmeg

3 cups milk or half-and-half

1 teaspoon vanilla extract

dash of salt

3 cups fresh or frozen blueberries

1½ cups pecans

⅓ cup butter or margarine

¾ cup brown sugar

Brunch Strata

Make the evening before! It's healthy and delicious for your family and guests.

Lightly grease a 9x13-inch baking pan.

Trim the crust from the bread and place the crusts in the bottom of the prepared pan. Layer with cheese, broccoli, and mushrooms over the crust and arrange the bread on top.

In a separate bowl, combine the eggs, milk, onion, and salt. Pour the egg and milk mixture over the bread. Cover and refrigerate overnight.

In the morning preheat oven to 325°. Bake for 55 minutes. Let stand 10 minutes before serving.

Note: Diced ham can also be added to this dish if desired.

Serves 12

12 slices white bread

12 ounces sharp cheddar cheese, sliced

2 (10-ounce) packages frozen chopped broccoli, cooked and drained

2 cups (2 8-ounce cans) mushroom pieces

6 eggs, slightly beaten

3½ cups milk

2 tablespoons instant minced onion

½ teaspoon salt

Diane Brown - Distribution

CHOCOLATE CHIP ZUCCHINI BREAD

Heat oven to 350°. Spray two 5x9-inch loaf pans with nonstick spray. In a large bowl, mix the flour, baking soda, baking powder, salt, and cinnamon. In a separate bowl, mix the sugar, oil, eggs, and vanilla on low speed.

Add the flour mixture and zucchini and mix until blended. Fold in the chocolate chips and nuts. Pour half of the batter into each prepared pan. Bake for 50 to 60 minutes or until a toothpick comes out clean from the center of the bread. Cool before cutting.

Keith Kiess - Information Technology

Serves 6

3 cups flour, sifted
1 teaspoon baking soda
½ teaspoon baking powder
1 ½ teaspoons salt
1 ½ teaspoons cinnamon

1 ½ cups sugar
1 cup vegetable oil
3 large eggs
1 teaspoon vanilla extract
3 cups shredded zucchini
1 cup chocolate chips
½ cup chopped nuts (optional)

CRISPY WAFFLES

Crispy and delicious, these are truly the BEST waffles ever! My grandchildren love them. If you don't own a waffle iron… this is the reason to buy one!

Heat the waffle iron. Combine the baking mix, egg, club soda, and oil in a bowl, and beat with a wire whisk until smooth. Pour onto the waffle iron. Bake until golden brown. Serve with your favorite toppings.

Barbara Bradley Baekgaard - Founder and Co-owner

Serves 4

2 cups waffle baking mix (or Bisquick)
1 egg
1 ⅓ cups club soda
½ cup vegetable oil

Chilled Corn & Buttermilk Bisque with Crab

Serves 6

5 ears of corn

2 teaspoons butter

2 teaspoons chopped garlic

1 cup chopped onion

½ cup chopped celery

1 bay leaf

1 tablespoon chopped fresh thyme

pinch of cayenne pepper

pinch of black pepper

½ cup dry sherry wine

3 cups chicken broth

1 cup buttermilk

½ cup heavy cream

2 teaspoons kosher salt

12 ounces cooked crabmeat

2 tablespoons chopped fresh chives

A wonderfully-flavored summertime soup from friends Mike and Maureen Catalogna, owners of Catablu, a gourmet restaurant in Fort Wayne, Indiana.

Cook ears of corn, cool and cut kernels from the cob. Melt butter in a 2-quart sauce pan. Add garlic, onions, and celery and cook until soft. Add the cooked corn, bay leaf, thyme, cayenne pepper, and black pepper. Cook for another 2 minutes. Add the sherry wine and bring to a boil; simmer on low for 5 minutes. After the sherry has reduced, add the chicken broth. Bring to a boil; simmer on low for 30 minutes.

Remove from the stove and discard the bay leaf. Purée the soup in a blender a little at a time. Strain the soup through a small hole colander, then place in refrigerator to cool.

After the soup has cooled, add the buttermilk, cream, and salt. Whisk until combined. Pour the soup into serving bowls and divide the crabmeat between them. Sprinkle with chives and serve.

Mike and Maureen Catalogna - Friends

Clam Chowder

Serves 8

4 ounces bacon

1 onion, chopped

6 potatoes, peeled, chopped

1 ½ cups clam juice

2 (7-ounce) cans clams, undrained

2 chicken bouillon cubes

1 teaspoon salt

¾ teaspoon Worcestershire sauce

½ teaspoon Tabasco sauce

¼ teaspoon white pepper

6 tablespoons butter

1 cup flour

5 cups half-and-half or milk

Fry the bacon in a heavy stockpot until crisp. Remove the bacon to paper towels to drain. Add the onion to the drippings in the stockpot. Sauté for 5 minutes. Add the potatoes, clam juice, undrained clams, bouillon cubes, salt, Worcestershire sauce, Tabasco sauce, and white pepper. Simmer for 30 minutes. Reduce heat to low.

Melt the butter in a heavy saucepan. Whisk in the flour to form a roux. Add the half-and-half or milk. Cook for 10 minutes or until thickened, stirring constantly. Add to the clam mixture. Crumble the bacon and add to the chowder. Simmer over medium-low heat for 10 minutes.

Ladle into soup bowls. Garnish with oyster crackers and fresh parsley.

Joanie Byrne Hall - Granddaughter of Vera Bradley / Pennsylvania Sales Representative

Pictured opposite upper left: Sydney Colby, daughter of Kim Colby, VP Design and Campbell Miller, grandson of Patricia Miller

Pictured opposite lower right: Patricia Miller's daughter-in-law, Elizabeth and granddaughter Emma

Baked Southwestern Corn Dip

Serves 8

1 (15-ounce) can yellow corn

1 (2.25-ounce) can sliced black olives

1 (4-ounce) can chopped green chilies

1 medium fresh jalapeño chile (about 2 tablespoons chopped) or ½ small can, drained

2 roasted red peppers, chopped

1 cup Monterey Jack or Colby cheese

½ cup grated Parmesan cheese

1 cup mayonnaise

This is great for football games, get-togethers, and, of course, the infamous family reunion!

Heat oven to 350°. Grease a 9x13-inch baking pan. Put the corn, olives, and green chilies in a colander to drain. Combine the corn, olives, green chilies, jalapeño chile, red peppers, Monterey Jack or Colby cheese, Parmesan cheese, and mayonnaise in a large bowl and mix well. Pour into the prepared baking dish.

Bake for about 30 minutes or until top is bubbly. Serve with tortilla chips.

Julie Berghoff - Friend

Beer Cheese Dip

Serves 8

3 ounces cream cheese, softened

8 ounces sharp cheddar cheese, shredded

1 garlic clove, minced

1 tablespoon Worcestershire sauce

½ teaspoon dry mustard

¼ teaspoon cayenne pepper

¼ cup beer

These are a few of our favorite things!

Beat the cream cheese and cheddar cheese at medium speed in a mixing bowl until combined. Add the garlic, Worcestershire sauce, dry mustard, and cayenne pepper and beat well. Add the beer gradually, beating constantly. Spoon into a serving bowl. Chill, covered, for 1 hour. Serve with crusty bread or crackers.

Katie Burns - Friend

French Bread with Pesto Parmesan Spread

This is the perfect accompaniment to a summer dinner. Just wrap in foil and throw on the grill for a couple of minutes.

Process the cream cheese and butter in a food processor until smooth. Add the basil, parsley, green onions, garlic, and Parmesan cheese and process to blend. Spoon into a small bowl. Chill, covered, in the refrigerator until ready to use.

Preheat oven to broil. Spread the cream cheese mixture on the bread slices. Sprinkle with additional Parmesan cheese. Sprinkle with cayenne pepper. Place on a baking sheet. Broil until the edges begin to brown. Serve immediately.

Renee Long - Marketing

Serves 6

8 ounces cream cheese, softened

¼ cup (½ stick) butter, softened

½ cup chopped fresh basil

2 tablespoons chopped fresh parsley

3 green onions with tops, thinly sliced

1 garlic clove, chopped

¼ cup freshly grated Parmesan cheese

1 loaf French bread, cut into ¼-inch slices

cayenne pepper to taste

lakeside fun

FRUIT SALSA WITH CINNAMON CRISPS

Every time I make this, people love it. It's so pretty and colorful and great on chicken or fish. If you plan to chill this salsa for more than 6 hours, stir in the strawberries just before serving.

In a mixing bowl, combine the strawberries, orange, kiwi, pineapple, green onions, sweet pepper, lime or lemon juice, and jalapeño. Cover and chill for 6 to 24 hours. Serve with Cinnamon Crisps.

Serves 24

1 cup finely chopped strawberries

1 medium orange, peeled and finely chopped

2 large or 3 small kiwi, peeled and finely chopped

½ cup finely chopped fresh pineapple or 1 (8-ounce) can crushed pineapple (juice pack), drained

¼ cup thinly sliced green onions

¼ cup finely chopped yellow or green sweet pepper

1 tablespoon lime or lemon juice

1 fresh jalapeño chile, seeded and chopped (optional)

Cinnamon Crisps (below)

CINNAMON CRISPS

Heat oven to 350°. Line a baking sheet with parchment. Brush the melted butter over the tortillas (or spray with butter spray). Combine the sugar and cinnamon in a pie plate and mix well, then place the tortillas one at a time butter-side down in the mixture. Cut each tortilla into wedges (as thick or thin as you'd like). Place the wedges in a single layer on baking sheet. Bake 5 to 10 minutes, or until crisp and lightly browned. Repeat with remaining wedges. Store in an airtight container at room temperature up to 4 days or in the freezer up to 3 weeks.

¼ cup melted butter or non-fat butter spray

12 8-inch flour tortillas

½ cup sugar

1 teaspoon ground cinnamon

Meghan Britton - Friend

Pictured opposite above: Maggie Byrne and John Ray

Opposite lower left: John Ray, Olivia Ray, Maggie Byrne

Opposite lower right: Barbara and Peer Baekgaard and their grandchildren John Ray, Maggie Byrne, Teddy and Molly Ray

POTATO PIZZA

Phyllo dough makes this easy recipe special.

Serves 6

½ package frozen phyllo dough

8 ounces cream cheese, softened
3 tablespoons milk
1 teaspoon basil
1 teaspoon oregano
salt and pepper to taste
6 medium red potatoes, parboiled
1 yellow pepper, diced
1 red pepper, diced
½ cup bacon bits
8 ounces smoked provolone cheese,
   thinly sliced

Heat oven to 400°. Line a cookie sheet with parchment. Unfold the package of phyllo dough, using only half the package. Freeze the remaining dough for another use. Using enough flour for dusting, roll the dough out to fit a standard cookie sheet. Place phyllo dough on the cookie sheet.

In a small bowl, blend the cream cheese, milk, and spices together until smooth. Spread over phyllo dough. Slice the parboiled potatoes very thin and place on top of the cream cheese mixture. Top with the peppers, bacon bits, and cheese. Bake for 12 to 15 minutes, or until cheese is bubbly. Cut into squares and serve.

Beckie Hollenbeck - Merchandising

ROASTED RED PEPPER DIP

Nancy Graham was hosting one of our famous Customer Service get-togethers and I volunteered to make this. It was so good that everyone wanted the recipe. Very tasty!

Serves 8

2 red bell peppers
1 (4-ounce) jar oil-pack sun-dried tomatoes
2 garlic cloves
2 teaspoons cumin
¼ cup chopped fresh cilantro
1 to 2 pickled jalapeño chiles, coarsely
   chopped
1 bunch green onions, white part only,
   chopped
6 ounces cream cheese, softened
½ teaspoon salt

Heat oven to broil. Cut the bell peppers into halves and discard the seeds. Place cut side down on a baking sheet. Broil until the tops are black. Place in a non-recycled brown paper bag or a sealable plastic food storage bag. Let stand for 10 to 15 minutes. Remove the skin from the bell peppers. Cool and press peppers between paper towels to remove excess moisture.

Drain the tomatoes and pat dry. Process the roasted bell peppers, tomatoes, garlic, cumin, cilantro, chiles, green onions, cream cheese, and salt in a food processor until smooth. Adjust the seasonings, adding additional jalapeño chiles if desired. Serve with blue corn chips.

Note: You may use one 4-ounce jar of roasted peppers instead of roasting your own peppers.

Phyllis Loy - Customer Service

SALSA-BAKED GOAT CHEESE

I find this recipe to be very versatile. It's one of the easiest summer appetizers for a group—full of flavor and delicious! I like to serve it with toasted pita chips, but my husband says it is best with the scoop style tortilla chips.

Heat oven to 350°. Spread nuts evenly on a baking sheet and toast them in the oven until lightly browned and very fragrant, about 6 to 7 minutes. Remove them from the oven and let cool.

In a medium bowl, combine the goat cheese and cream cheese together using a fork. Add the green onions and shape into a ball. Roll the cheese ball in the toasted pecans. Place in the center of a 9-inch decorative pie plate. Bake the cheese ball for about 6 minutes. Spoon salsa over heated cheese ball and return to the oven for another 3 minutes. Remove from the oven and sprinkle with cilantro. Serve immediately with toasted pita chips.

Stefanie Chevillet - Friend

Serves 6

¼ cup chopped pecans

1 (4-ounce) package goat cheese

1 (8-ounce) package cream cheese, softened

1 bunch green onions, chopped

1 cup roasted jalapeño salsa, or your favorite variety

1 tablespoon finely chopped cilantro

SAVORY CHEESE BISCUITS

These pair well with seafood.

Heat oven to 425°. Grease and flour a 9x13 baking sheet. Sift together flour, baking powder, salt, and dry mustard; cut in butter. Stir in shredded cheese, parsley, and milk. Mix together lightly with a fork, just until moistened. Turn dough out onto a floured surface and knead gently a few times, until smooth.

Roll out about ¾-inch thick and cut with round biscuit cutter, or drop by tablespoons onto baking sheet. Brush tops with milk. Bake 20 to 25 minutes, or until browned.

Melissa Cordial - Marketing

Makes 1 dozen

2 cups all-purpose flour, sifted before measuring

2 ½ teaspoons baking powder

½ teaspoon salt

½ teaspoon dry mustard

3 tablespoons butter

⅔ cup shredded sharp cheddar cheese

2 tablespoons minced fresh parsley

½ cup milk

⅛ cup milk

summertime salsa

SUMMERTIME SALSA

In Hampton, we all love watermelon. Our claim to fame is the Hampton County Watermelon Festival, the longest continuing festival in South Carolina. This watermelon salsa is especially good on grilled chicken and fish. Enjoy!

Mix watermelon, onion, cilantro, jalapeño chile, lime juice, and brown sugar in a bowl until blended. Let rest at least 30 minutes at room temperature before serving.

Serve with tortilla chips.

Reba Peeples and Rebecca Young - Retailers (The Frock Shop, Hampton, South Carolina)

Serves 6 to 8

4 cups diced watermelon

1 small red onion, finely chopped

½ bunch fresh cilantro, chopped

1 jalapeño chile, diced

juice of 1 lime

pinch of brown sugar

recipe hint

Cilantro, also called Chinese parsley, is used a great deal in Asian and Latin American cooking. It cools spicy foods and has a unique flavor and aroma.

WARM SWISS CHEESE AND BACON DIP

Heat oven to 350°. Combine the cream cheese, Swiss cheese, mayonnaise, and green onions in a bowl and mix well. Spoon into a small baking dish. Bake for 20 minutes. Sprinkle with the bacon bits and cracker crumbs. Serve warm with crackers.

Note: You may substitute ½ cup sliced almonds for the butter cracker crumbs for a different twist.

Nancy Graham - Friend

Serves 8

8 ounces cream cheese, softened

1 cup grated Swiss cheese

½ cup mayonnaise

2 tablespoons chopped green onions

½ cup bacon bits

½ cup butter cracker crumbs

Chicken Pasta Salad

Serves 8 to 10

1 pound rotelle or other spiral pasta

4 whole skinless boneless chicken breasts, poached and cut into bite-size pieces

20 cherry tomatoes, quartered

8 green onions with tops, thinly sliced

4 tablespoons finely chopped fresh basil

salt and pepper to taste

1 cup sugar snap peas

Creamy Curry Dressing (below)

Zesty, spicy, and ooh, so good. This salad is great to take to a summer picnic or to serve as an easy mid-week dinner.

In a large pot of boiling water, cook the pasta for 10 minutes or until tender. Drain in a colander and rinse with cold water. Drain well. In a large bowl, combine the pasta, chicken, tomatoes, green onions, and basil. Season with salt and pepper. Set aside.

Fill a small stockpot ¾ full of water and bring to a boil. Add sugar snap peas and blanch for 1 minute or until they turn bright green. Drain, rinse under cold water, and cut peas in half.

Add the Creamy Curry Dressing to the pasta mixture, stirring to combine. Fold in sugar snap peas and serve when ready.

Creamy Curry Dressing

4 tablespoons unsalted butter

2 teaspoons minced garlic

4 teaspoons minced, peeled fresh ginger root

1 cup heavy whipping cream

4 tablespoons apple cider vinegar

3 teaspoons curry powder

pinch of dried hot red pepper flakes to taste

4 tablespoons Major Grey's Chutney

Melt the butter in a medium-sized skillet. Add garlic and ginger root. Cook over moderately low heat, stirring until the garlic is softened. Add the cream and cook the mixture until it is slightly thickened. Remove from heat and whisk in vinegar, curry powder, red pepper flakes, and chutney.

Kathy Reedy Ray - Granddaughter of Vera Bradley / Michigan Sales Representative

Chop House Coleslaw

Serves 10

1 package red cabbage

4 (16-ounce) packages coleslaw mix

1 jar bleu cheese salad dressing

salt and pepper to taste

This is very easy to make, requiring few ingredients, and it's always a welcome surprise and a great twist to traditional coleslaw! Great for picnics, tailgating and barbeques!

Mix red cabbage, coleslaw, bleu cheese dressing, salt and pepper in a large bowl. Chill, covered, until ready to serve.

Note: For optional twists, you may add cucumber slices, crumbled bacon bits, and/or diced tomatoes.

Patti Reedy Parker - Granddaughter of Vera Bradley / North & South Carolina Sales Representative

chop house coleslaw

corn salad

CORN SALAD

This is best made with fresh corn, if you can get it.

In a large skillet over medium-high heat, add the butter and oil. Sauté the corn until roasted. In a medium bowl, combine the onion, vinegar, olive oil, basil, and roasted corn. Mix well. Add salt and pepper to taste.

Note: I use sea salt and we like a lot of it.

Leslie Byrne - Daughter-in-law of Barbara Bradley Baekgaard

Serves 6

1 tablespoon butter
1 tablespoon vegetable oil
1 package frozen white corn

½ red onion, chopped
3 tablespoons apple cider vinegar
3 tablespoons olive oil
1 to 2 tablespoons chopped fresh basil
salt and pepper to taste

CREOLE POTATO SALAD

Cook the potatoes in enough boiling salted water to cover for 12 minutes or until tender; drain and cool slightly.

Combine mayonnaise, Creole mustard, vinegar, salt, horseradish, thyme, garlic powder, and cayenne pepper in a large bowl. Add the potatoes, egg, and onion, tossing gently. Serve immediately or chill for future use.

Cheri Lantz - Sales

Serves 8

3 pounds red potatoes, cubed

½ cup mayonnaise
½ cup Creole mustard
1 tablespoon red wine vinegar
1 teaspoon salt
1 teaspoon prepared horseradish
½ teaspoon thyme
¼ teaspoon garlic powder
¼ teaspoon cayenne pepper
6 hard-cooked eggs, chopped
1 medium sweet onion, diced

recipe hint

Do you cover vegetables when cooking or not? As a general rule, root vegetables (those that grow underground) should be covered while being cooked. Those veggies that grow above ground, being more delicate, should be cooked uncovered.

1 cup trimmed green beans

1 cup trimmed asparagus

1 (16-ounce) can quartered artichoke
hearts, drained

1 (15-ounce) can kidney beans, drained

1 (16-ounce) package baby carrots, sliced

2 medium red onions, chopped

1 medium red bell pepper, chopped

1 medium yellow bell pepper, chopped

¾ cup olive oil

½ cup red wine vinegar

¼ cup sugar

salt and pepper to taste

EIGHT-VEGETABLE
MARINATED SALAD

Steam the green beans and asparagus over a large pot of salted water for 3 to 4 minutes until just crisp and tender. Drain and rinse with cold water. Cut asparagus spears into 1-inch pieces. Combine green beans, asparagus, artichoke hearts, kidney beans, carrots, onions, red pepper, and yellow pepper in a large serving bowl.

In a small mixing bowl, combine the olive oil, vinegar, and sugar and whisk well. Pour over vegetables and stir gently. Season with salt and pepper. Cover and marinate in the refrigerator for 8 to 12 hours. Serve at room temperature.

Kathy Reedy Ray - Granddaughter of Vera Bradley / Michigan Sales Representative

Serves 8

⅔ cup olive oil

⅓ cup cider vinegar

6 green onions, white part only, sliced

1 tablespoon chopped fresh parsley

1 tablespoon chopped fresh chives

1 tablespoon stone ground mustard

2 teaspoons honey

2 teaspoons lemon zest

salt and pepper to taste

3 pounds small red-skinned potatoes,
quartered

8 bacon slices or ¼ cup real bacon bits

12 Romaine lettuce leaves

½ cup crumbled bleu cheese

1 hard-cooked egg, diced

POTATO SALAD WITH
BLEU CHEESE AND BACON

A full-flavored version of a traditional summer dish.

To make the dressing: Whisk the oil, vinegar, green onions, parsley, chives, mustard, honey, and lemon zest in a large bowl until well blended. Season dressing with salt and pepper.

Cook the potatoes in a large pot of boiling salted water, about 8 to 10 minutes, or until tender. Drain. Add warm potatoes to dressing. Toss to combine.

Cook the bacon in a large skillet over medium heat until crisp. Drain on paper towels. Crumble into small pieces. Arrange the lettuce leaves on a large platter. Mound potato salad in center of platter. Sprinkle with bacon, bleu cheese, and egg. Serve at room temperature.

Debbie Wilson - Administration

Pictured: Stefanie and Chip Chevillet, friends of Vera Bradley

Fourth of July

Summertime Pasta Salad

Common ingredients, easy to make, great for unexpected guests.

Cook the pasta according to package directions. Drain. In a large bowl, combine pasta, spinach, onion, tomatoes, cucumbers, olives, feta cheese, and Parmesan cheese. Mix well.

In a small bowl, whisk the olive oil, vinegar, mustard, and Parmesan cheese. Pour vinaigrette over pasta salad and mix well. Add salt and pepper to taste. This salad is best made 1 day in advance to allow flavors to blend.

Kathy Reedy Ray - Granddaughter of Vera Bradley / Michigan Sales Representative

Serves a crowd

1 (16-ounce) box tubular pasta

1 bunch spinach, cleaned and torn into bite-sized pieces

1 large red onion, diced

2 large tomatoes, chopped

2 medium cucumbers, peeled, seeded, and diced

1 small can sliced olives, drained

1 (16-ounce) package feta cheese, crumbled

¼ cup shredded Parmesan cheese

¾ cup olive oil

⅓ cup red wine vinegar

2 tablespoons Dijon mustard

1 tablespoon Parmesan cheese

salt and freshly ground pepper to taste

helpful hint

If you grow your own tomatoes and a fall frost threatens, here's what to do. Just pull the whole tomato plant up out of the dirt – roots and all – and hang it somewhere out of sight. The remaining green tomatoes will continue to ripen and give you one more month of summer.

BAKED VIDALIA ONIONS

These onions are a great accompaniment to grilled steaks or pork chops.

Heat oven to 400°. Cut each onion in quarters, cutting to but not through the bottom. Place ¼ tablespoon butter on each quarter and 1 bouillon cube in the center of each onion. Sprinkle with Parmesan cheese, salt and pepper. Wrap each onion individually in foil. Bake for 1 hour. Unwrap the onions and serve immediately.

Nancy Graham - Friend

Serves 4

4 medium to large Vidalia onions
¼ cup (½ stick) butter or margarine
4 beef or chicken bouillon cubes
½ cup grated Parmesan cheese
salt and pepper to taste

CHIP'S GRILLED POTATOES

We cook these potatoes quite often in the summer. They are delicious and there is no mess to clean up afterward.

Prepare grill. Combine the potatoes, onion, celery, and bacon in a medium bowl and toss to mix well. Place on a large piece of foil coated with nonstick cooking spray.

Whisk the oil, cornstarch, rosemary, thyme, salt and pepper together. Drizzle over the potato mixture. Top with another piece of foil sprayed with nonstick cooking spray. Seal the edges to form a packet.

Place on a grill rack. Grill over hot coals for 1 hour. The potatoes will cook evenly so there is no need to turn over the packet.

Stefanie Chevillet - Friend

Serves 6

6 medium potatoes, chopped
1 medium onion, chopped
2 ribs celery, chopped
2 slices bacon, chopped

½ cup olive oil
2 tablespoons cornstarch
rosemary, thyme, salt and pepper to taste

DANISH RED CABBAGE

My husband Peer was born and raised in Copenhagen, Denmark. Of all of his mother's recipes, this was one of his favorites. I often serve it with Lila's Chicken (page 34).

In a large saucepan over medium-high heat, melt the butter. Add sugar and stir until dissolved. Add cabbage and sauté briefly. Stir in vinegar. Simmer, covered, for 1 hour, adding water as needed to prevent burning. Watch carefully. Add the jelly and mix well. Simmer, covered, for 20 to 25 minutes. Adjust the vinegar and jelly to taste. Serve immediately.

Barbara Bradley Baekgaard - Founder and Co-owner

Serves 8

3 tablespoons butter

2 tablespoons sugar

1 medium head red cabbage, thinly sliced

¼ cup white vinegar

1 (6-ounce) jar red currant jelly

entertaining hint

An easy way to serve butter for corn-on-the-cob is to cut small squares of bread and top them with a pat of butter. This is much easier than trying to butter corn with a knife as the butter melts away too quickly. And your guests can eat the bread too. (Pictured at left.)

ROASTED BELL PEPPER PASTA

The fennel seeds and roasted peppers give this pasta dish a meaty flavor.

In a large nonstick skillet, heat the oil over medium heat. Add the onions, fennel seeds, and garlic. Cook, covered, for 10 minutes, stirring occasionally. Add the tomatoes. Bring to a boil and reduce heat. Simmer, uncovered, for 30 minutes, stirring occasionally.

Cut the roasted bell peppers into julienne strips. Add to the tomato mixture. Season with salt and pepper. Cook for 3 minutes or until heated through.

Combine the cooked pasta, roasted pepper mixture, and basil in a large serving bowl and toss to mix well. Sprinkle with the Parmesan cheese. Serve immediately.

Joan Bradley Reedy - Daughter of Vera Bradley / South Carolina Sales Representative

Serves 8

1 tablespoon olive oil

2 cups chopped onions

½ teaspoon fennel seeds, crushed

2 garlic cloves, minced

2 (14-ounce) cans chopped tomatoes

2 green bell peppers, roasted

2 red bell peppers, roasted

2 yellow bell peppers, roasted

½ teaspoon salt

¼ teaspoon pepper

6 ½ cups tubular or bow-tie pasta, cooked, drained

½ cup thinly sliced fresh basil

½ cup grated Parmesan cheese

Makes 12 cakes

1 pound lump crabmeat

½ cup chopped roasted red peppers

3 green onions, chopped

2 tablespoons mayonnaise

1 tablespoon Dijon mustard

1 ⅓ cups bread crumbs

dash of cayenne pepper

salt and pepper to taste

2 egg yolks, beaten

1 cup flour

2 egg whites, slightly beaten

1 ⅔ cups bread crumbs

2 tablespoons butter

Basil Aioli (below)

¾ cup mayonnaise

⅓ cup chopped fresh basil

1 tablespoon lemon juice

1 ½ teaspoons minced garlic

1 ½ teaspoons lemon zest

ANNAPOLIS CRAB CAKES

This is a Maryland tradition.

Combine the crabmeat, peppers, green onion, mayonnaise, and mustard in a bowl. Mix in bread crumbs, cayenne pepper, salt and pepper. Stir in the egg yolks.

For each cake, shape ⅓ cup crab mixture into a patty. Dredge in flour and shake off the excess. Brush the cakes with the egg whites, and coat with bread crumbs. Chill, covered, in the refrigerator for 2 to 6 hours.

Melt butter in a pan over medium heat. Cook the crab cakes until golden brown, approximately 4 minutes per side. Serve with Basil Aioli.

BASIL AIOLI

You'll probably want to double this recipe, as it goes quickly.

Combine mayonnaise, basil, lemon juice, garlic, and lemon zest in a bowl and stir until smooth.

Donna Watson - Maryland Sales Representative

seaside dinner

Serves 6 to 8

2 ½ tablespoons paprika

2 tablespoons salt

2 tablespoons garlic powder

1 tablespoon black pepper

1 tablespoon onion powder

1 tablespoon cayenne pepper

1 tablespoon oregano

1 tablespoon thyme

3 to 4 pounds thick-cut country-style pork ribs

1 cup cider vinegar

2 to 3 tablespoons butter

1 tablespoon fresh lemon juice

1 teaspoon onion powder

2 cloves garlic, minced

salt and pepper to taste

COUNTRY PORK RIBS

These are a speciality at the Sawyers household.

To make dry rub: In a small bowl combine the paprika, salt, garlic powder, black pepper, onion powder, cayenne pepper, oregano, and thyme. (You can substitute a pre-made spicy rub.) Apply the rub generously to all sides of the ribs, and let stand for 30 minutes at room temperature.

To make mop sauce: Combine vinegar, butter, lemon juice, onion powder, garlic, salt and pepper in a saucepan and heat on stove until butter is melted.

Prepare grill for indirect heating at no more than 275° to 300°, or place the ribs on a roasting rack in the oven at the same temperature. Cook the ribs until the internal temperature registers 160°, at least 2 hours. Baste the ribs every 20 minutes with the mop sauce. Once the ribs are cooked, apply your favorite barbeque sauce and cook another 5 minutes.

Mark Sawyers - Accounting

recipe hint

When grilling, never poke meat with a fork to turn it over. Use tongs so the juice stays inside where it belongs. And why not barbeque a little bit extra? When it's done, pop it from the grill before anyone notices, wrap it in foil and freeze. A few days later thaw and heat. Everyone will think you've been toiling in the heat to bring them that great summer taste. We won't tell if you won't.

Fillet of Beef with Gorgonzola Sauce

Serves 8 to 10

Heat oven to 400°. Place the beef on a cookie sheet. Mix the salt, pepper, and mustard in a small bowl. Using your hands, coat beef with mustard mixture. Roast in the oven 30 minutes for rare or 40 minutes for medium to medium-rare.

Remove meat from the oven and tent with aluminum foil. Allow meat to set for 15 minutes. Meat will continue to cook while setting.

For the Gorgonzola sauce, place the cheese in the bowl of a food processor fitted with a steel blade and process. Add the cream cheese, mayonnaise, sour cream, green onions, salt, pepper, and Worcestershire sauce. Process until smooth. Serve at room temperature.

Stefanie Chevillet - Friend

1 whole fillet of beef, 4 to 5 pounds, trimmed

kosher salt to taste
black pepper to taste
½ cup stone ground mustard

6 ounces Gorgonzola cheese
8 ounces cream cheese, softened
½ cup mayonnaise
½ cup sour cream
1 bunch green onions, green parts only, trimmed and sliced,
1 teaspoon kosher salt
freshly ground black pepper to taste
¼ teaspoon Worcestershire sauce

Flank Steak with Marinade

Serves 4

As children, we always requested this meal for our "birthday dinners." There were six children in our family, so we were able to have it quite often. It is still a favorite at cookouts and get-togethers, especially when my friends are home from Florida.

In a glass jar, mix the soy sauce, oil, garlic, ginger, mustard and molasses. Let marinade stand for 2 hours.

Place the flank steak in a shallow baking dish. Pour the marinade over the steak. Chill, covered, in the refrigerator for 6 to 8 hours. Prepare the grill and cook the steak for 4 to 6 minutes per side.

Sally Pietzak - Human Resources

⅔ cup soy sauce
¼ cup oil
6 cloves garlic, minced
2 teaspoons ginger
2 teaspoons dry mustard
2 tablespoons molasses
2 pounds flank steak

Gregory's Jamaican White Fish

One of Gregory's mamma's favorite recipes!

Heat oven to 350°. Lightly grease a 9x13 baking dish. Lightly salt and pepper the fish fillets. Let them set for 15 minutes.

In a small bowl, combine curry powder, onion, green pepper, and olive oil. Coat the fillets with this mixture. Place the fish in the prepared baking dish. Bake for 15 to 20 minutes.

Serve the fish over white rice.

Gregory Phillpotts - Friend

Serves 4 to 6

2 pounds white fish fillets (walleye, tilapia, cod)

salt and pepper to taste

3 tablespoons yellow curry powder
¼ cup finely chopped onion
¼ cup finely chopped green pepper
1 tablespoon olive oil

3 cups cooked white rice

recipe hint

Thoroughly cooked fish are opaque and have milky juices. Poke them with a fork at the thickest part of the filet to see if they begin to flake easily. Fish that are translucent, with clear juices, are not fully cooked.

GRILLED CHICKEN

The marinade makes this grilled chicken very tender and quite delicious.

Place the chicken in a shallow glass dish. In a large glass measure, combine the oil, soy sauce, vinegar, Worcestershire sauce, lemon juice, garlic, dry mustard, parsley, salt and pepper and mix well. Pour over the chicken. Marinate, covered, in the refrigerator for 8 to 12 hours.

Prepare grill.

Drain the chicken, reserving the marinade. Place the reserved marinade in a small saucepan. Bring to a boil. Boil for 2 to 3 minutes, stirring constantly. Place the chicken on the grill rack. Grill over medium hot coals for 5 to 6 minutes. Brush both sides with the cooked marinade. Grill for 5 minutes longer or until the juices run clear.

Patti Pine - Sales

Serves 4 to 6

4 to 6 chicken breasts

½ cup vegetable oil
⅓ cup soy sauce
¼ cup white wine vinegar
2 tablespoons Worcestershire sauce
¼ cup lemon juice
1 garlic clove, crushed
1 tablespoon dry mustard
½ tablespoon parsley
½ teaspoon salt
pepper to taste

SPICE-CRUSTED SALMON WITH SALSA

Combine the oranges, onion, lime juice, cilantro, chiles, garlic, salt and pepper in a bowl and toss to mix well. Chill salsa, covered, in the refrigerator until ready to use.

Prepare grill or heat oven to broil. Mix the coriander seeds, cumin seeds, peppercorns, and kosher salt in a small bowl. Rub on the fish. Place on a grill or broiler rack. Grill or broil for 4 minutes per side or until the fish flakes easily. Serve immediately with the salsa.

Lyn Killoran - Friend

Serves 4

4 navel oranges, peeled and sectioned
1 small red onion, finely chopped
¼ cup fresh lime juice
¼ cup chopped fresh cilantro
1 tablespoon minced jalapeño chiles
1 garlic clove, minced
salt and pepper to taste

1 tablespoon coriander seeds, crushed
1 tablespoon cumin seeds, crushed
½ tablespoon black peppercorns
1 teaspoon kosher salt

4 salmon fillets, skinned

SUMMER SHRIMP BOIL

Serves 6

3 quarts water

½ cup Old Bay Seasoning

18 small red potatoes, cleaned

6 Italian sausage links, cut in thirds (sweet, mild, or hot according to your taste)

6 ears fresh corn on the cob, broken in halves

3 pounds large fresh shrimp, unpeeled

cocktail sauce
crusty bread

This recipe is so popular in our home that we have a special seafood-themed platter and matching dishes just for serving it! Add a pitcher of your favorite summertime cocktail and any ordinary summer evening becomes a festive occasion.

In a large stockpot, bring the water and Old Bay Seasoning to a boil. Add potatoes, return to boil and cook until almost tender. Add sausage and corn on the cob. Cook 10 minutes.

Remove potatoes, corn, and sausage with a slotted spoon to a large serving platter and cover with aluminum foil to keep warm. Add shrimp to stockpot. Cook 3 to 5 minutes or until shrimp turns pink.

Remove shrimp with a slotted spoon to platter. Sprinkle the food with a little more Old Bay Seasoning and serve with cocktail sauce and the sliced loaf of crusty bread.

Note: This recipe can easily be modified to serve more or less people—just adjust the proportions. Per person, you need 3 potatoes, 1 sausage link, 1 ear of corn and a ½ pound of shrimp.

Yvonne Marson - West Virginia Sales Representative

WHISKEY BARBEQUE RIBS

Serves 6

1 cup ketchup

1 cup Jack Daniel's Whiskey

1 cup brown sugar

½ cup finely chopped onion

2 tablespoons Worcestershire sauce

2 tablespoons hot sauce

1 tablespoon Dijon mustard

1 clove garlic, minced

2 tablespoons (¼ stick) butter

pinch of fennel seeds

4 pounds baby-back ribs

Amazing ribs... you have to try these!

Heat oven to 300°. In a saucepan, combine the ketchup, whiskey, brown sugar, onion, Worcestershire sauce, hot sauce, Dijon mustard, garlic, butter, and fennel seeds. Bring to a boil and simmer for 30 minutes. Makes about 2 ½ cups of barbeque sauce.

Rub the ribs in the barbeque sauce and wrap in foil. Bake for 3 hours.

Jim Berghoff - Friend

whiskey barbeque ribs

berry cream pie

Berry Cream Pie

Sugar cream pie meets fresh berries. What could be sweeter?

Heat oven to 425°. Cream together sugar, flour, and butter. Add salt, heavy cream, and milk. Pour into unbaked pie shell.

Arrange fresh blueberries or raspberries on top. For a more formal look, use both kinds of berries and alternate rows.

Bake for 10 minutes, then reduce the temperature to 350°. Bake for 40 minutes or until middle appears set. Cover the crust with foil mid-way through baking if it appears to be over browning. Serve chilled.

Amy Byrne Ray - Granddaughter of Vera Bradley

Serves 6 to 8

1 cup sugar

½ cup flour

1 tablespoon butter

⅛ teaspoon salt

1 cup heavy cream

½ cup milk

1 9-inch pie shell, unbaked

1 pint raspberries and/or blueberries

Georgia Chess Pie

My mom always made this pie for me as I was growing up. She got up early every Sunday morning and made pie before going to church. We'd have a big meal after church, topped off with Georgia Chess Pie! I'm not sure how or where my mother discovered this recipe, but I'm sure glad she did. It's the best pie in the world!

Heat oven to 325°. Cream the margarine, vanilla, and sugar together, then add the eggs 1 at a time. Add the cornmeal, vinegar, and cornstarch and mix well. Stir in the coconut. Pour into unbaked pie shell. Bake for 1 hour.

Todd Shinabarger - Information Technology

Serves 6 to 8

½ cup (1 stick) margarine

1 tablespoon vanilla extract

1½ cups sugar

3 eggs

1 teaspoon cornmeal

1 teaspoon vinegar

1 teaspoon cornstarch

1 cup coconut

1 (9-inch) pie shell, unbaked

Giant Chocolate Chip Cookies

Makes 3 dozen

4 ½ cups flour

2 teaspoons baking soda

1 teaspoon salt

1 cup (2 sticks) unsalted butter, softened

1 cup vegetable shortening

1 ½ cups sugar

1 ½ cups brown sugar

2 tablespoons sour cream

1 tablespoon vanilla extract

4 large eggs

2 (12-ounce) packages semisweet chocolate chips

I have made a lot of chocolate chip cookies in my life, but these are definitely the best!

Heat oven to 350°. Sift the flour, baking soda, and salt into a medium bowl. Using an electric mixer, beat the butter and shortening in a large bowl until fluffy. Add the sugar, brown sugar, sour cream, and vanilla, and beat to blend. Beat in eggs 1 at a time, then add the flour mixture. Fold in chocolate chips.

Drop batter by heaping tablespoons onto an ungreased cookie sheet—about 2 tablespoons of batter per cookie. You can bake 6 cookies per baking sheet.

Bake until golden brown, about 14 minutes, rotating cookie sheets halfway through. Cool on cookie sheets for 5 minutes. Transfer cookies to wire racks to cool completely.

Note: For our cookbook, we made these into large ice cream sandwiches, pictured right.

Barbara Bradley Baekgaard - Founder and Co-owner

Happy Oatmeal Cookies

Makes 3 dozen

1 cup (2 sticks) unsalted butter, melted

1 ½ cups brown sugar

¾ cup granulated sugar

2 eggs

1 tablespoon vanilla extract

1 ½ cups unbleached flour

1 teaspoon baking soda

1 tablespoon cinnamon

3 cups rolled oats

1 ½ cups raisins

These cookies remind me of home, warmth and love. The ultimate comfort food! There are many reasons people love to bake cookies. My little reasons are Alex, Catie, Bella, and Noah.

Heat oven to 350°. With an electric mixer, cream the butter, brown sugar and granulated sugar in a mixing bowl. Add the eggs and vanilla and mix well. Add the flour, baking soda, and cinnamon and mix well. Fold in the oats and raisins.

Drop cookie dough by heaping spoonfuls onto an ungreased cookie sheet. Bake for 11 to 13 minutes, or until lightly browned. Let the cookies cool on the sheet for a few minutes before removing to a wire rack.

Heidi Floyd - Customer Service

Pictured opposite:
John and Teddy Ray with Maggie Byrne enjoying their ice cream sandwiches

HILLSBORO CLUB
BLUEBERRY COOKIES

Makes 3 dozen

2 ½ cups flour
1 teaspoon baking powder
1 teaspoon salt

1 cup (2 sticks) butter, softened
¾ cup sugar
¾ cup brown sugar
2 large eggs, slightly beaten
½ cup dried blueberries

sugar

We photographed our Spring 2006 Vera Bradley catalog in south Florida. Martha, the wonderful chef, made these cookies for us. We asked if we could have this recipe for our cookbook, and here it is. Enjoy!

Heat oven to 350°. Coat cookie sheet with nonstick cooking spray. In a medium mixing bowl, sift together flour, baking powder, and salt. Set aside. In a separate bowl, using an electric mixer, beat butter until creamy. Add sugar and brown sugar and beat until light and fluffy. Beat in eggs 1 at a time. Add blueberries. Gradually add in flour mixture until thoroughly combined.

Drop by rounded teaspoonfuls onto a cookie sheet. Bake for 10 minutes. Remove from oven and let cool on baking sheet. While cookies are cooling, sprinkle each with additional sugar. After 5 minutes, remove to wire racks to complete cooling.

Barbara Bradley Baekgaard - Founder and Co-owner

recipe hint

Baking powder begins to work as soon as it encounters liquid, so recipes that include it should be baked as quickly as possible after mixing.

INDIANA MINT BROWNIES

This is one recipe that I have called on over the years for numerous occasions… from birthdays to carry-ins. I like this dessert because it's very rich and moist. Don't be surprised if someone asks for the recipe!

Heat oven to 350°. Grease a 9x13-inch cake pan. With an electric mixer, beat butter and sugar in a large mixing bowl until light and fluffy. Add the eggs, chocolate syrup, and vanilla and beat well. Add the flour and salt and beat until smooth. Pour into cake pan. Bake 30 minutes or until a wooden pick inserted in the center comes out clean. Set on a wire rack to cool.

Cream butter and confectioners' sugar in a mixing bowl. Add the crème de menthe and beat well. Spread over the cooled brownies. Spread Chocolate Glaze over the top. Chill, covered, for 6 hours or longer. Cut into squares.

CHOCOLATE GLAZE

Melt the chocolate chips and butter in a small saucepan, stirring frequently. Remove from heat and cool slightly.

Diane Brown - Distribution

Makes 2 dozen

1 cup (2 sticks) butter or margarine, softened

1 cup sugar

4 eggs, lightly beaten

1 (16-ounce) can chocolate syrup

1 teaspoon vanilla extract

1 cup flour

½ teaspoon salt

½ cup (1 stick) butter or margarine, softened

2 cups confectioners' sugar

2 tablespoons crème de menthe

Chocolate Glaze (below)

1 cup chocolate chips

6 tablespoons butter or margarine

LEMON CAKE
WITH WHISKEY GLAZE

Serve this for brunch, afternoon tea, or as a summer dessert. When paired with ice cream, it's a real treat.

Heat oven to 350°. Butter and flour 10- to 12-cup tube or Bundt pan. Stir cake mix and pudding mix in a large bowl to blend. Beat in eggs 1 at a time, then the milk, whiskey, oil and lemon zest. Mix the nuts with flour in a small bowl; stir into batter. Pour into pan.

Bake until a toothpick inserted near the center comes out clean, about 50 minutes. Place pan on rack while preparing glaze.

Spoon hot Whiskey Glaze over the cake. Cool cake completely in the pan. Invert on serving platter and cut into slices.

WHISKEY GLAZE

Stir sugar, butter, and whiskey in a heavy small saucepan over medium-low heat until butter melts, sugar dissolves, and syrup bubbles, about 5 minutes.

Stefanie Chevillet - Friend

Serves 12

1 (18.5 ounce) package yellow cake mix

1 (3.4 ounce) package instant lemon pudding mix

4 large eggs

1 cup milk (do not use low-fat or nonfat)

¼ cup whiskey

½ cup vegetable oil

1 tablespoon lemon zest

1 cup chopped pecans

2 teaspoons flour

Whiskey Glaze (below)

½ cup sugar

¼ cup (½ stick) unsalted butter

½ cup whiskey

MIXED BERRY CRISP

Serves 8

3 nectarines, chopped

1 cup blueberries

1 cup sliced strawberries

1 cup raspberries

¼ cup sugar

¼ cup flour

1 tablespoon fresh lemon juice

¾ cup flour

¾ cup old-fashioned oats

⅔ cup brown sugar

1 teaspoon cinnamon

½ teaspoon ginger

¼ teaspoon nutmeg

¼ teaspoon salt

7 tablespoons cold butter, cut into pieces

This berry crisp is great served warm with a big dollop of vanilla ice cream.

Heat oven to 375°. Combine the nectarines, blueberries, strawberries, raspberries, sugar, flour, and lemon juice in a large bowl and toss to mix well. Spoon into a 9-inch glass pie plate.

Mix the flour, oats, brown sugar, cinnamon, ginger, nutmeg, and salt in a bowl. Cut in the butter until crumbly. Sprinkle over the berry mixture.

Bake for 1 hour or until bubbly and the top is golden brown. Let stand for 15 minutes before servings. Serve warm or at room temperature.

Julie North - Human Resources

NECTARINE COCONUT CAKE

Serves 16

2 eggs

½ cup vegetable oil

⅔ cup honey

¾ cup plain yogurt

1 teaspoon vanilla extract

2 cups cake flour

1 teaspoon baking soda

1 cup shredded coconut

1 ½ cups fresh nectarine slices

6 tablespoons cinnamon

A summertime favorite at Vera Bradley.

Heat oven to 350°. Grease a 6-cup tube pan. Beat the eggs in a mixing bowl until pale yellow. Add the oil, honey, yogurt, and vanilla. Sift together cake flour and baking soda. Gradually add the flour mixture into the wet ingredients. Stir in the coconut.

Pour ¼ of the batter into the tube pan. Arrange ⅓ of the nectarine slices evenly over the batter. Sprinkle with 2 tablespoons of the cinnamon. Repeat the layers twice, alternating fruit with batter, ending with the batter.

Bake for 40 to 45 minutes or until a toothpick inserted in the center comes out clean. Store in the refrigerator.

Michael Nelaborige - Friend

RUTH'S ITALIAN POUND CAKE

When I was very pregnant with my third child, we went to a party where this was served. I consumed at least half of the cake. The next day Henry was born. As a "welcome home" gift, Ruth baked another cake for me and attached the recipe. Serve this with dinner, and the leftovers (if any) are great for breakfast.

Heat oven to 325°. Grease and flour a 10-cup tube or Bundt pan. With an electric mixer, beat the butter in a mixing bowl until light and fluffy. Add the sugar gradually, beating constantly. Beat in the oil and milk. Add the eggs 1 at a time, beating well after each addition.

In a separate bowl, sift together the flour and baking powder. Gradually beat flour mixture into the sugar mixture. Stir in the almond extract. Pour into pan. Bake for 90 minutes or until toothpick inserted in center comes out clean.

Joanie Byrne Hall - Granddaughter of Vera Bradley / Pennsylvania Sales Representative

Serves 16

¼ cup butter, softened

3 cups sugar

¼ cup vegetable oil

1 cup milk

6 eggs

3 cups flour

1 tablespoon baking powder

2 teaspoons almond extract

Green Tea Soda
with Fresh Fruit

A light and refreshing drink to beat the summer heat.

Boil the water and add tea bags. Let steep for 2 to 3 minutes. Remove tea bags and stir in the honey or sugar. Chill tea for at least 2 hours.

Fill 8 to 10 glasses about half full with tea. Add fruit to each glass and fill with ice and sparkling water. Top with fresh mint and a slice of lime.

Susan Britton - Friend

Serves 8 to 10

4 cups water

8 bags organic green tea

3 tablespoons honey or sugar

4 cups fresh summer fruit such as raspberries, blueberries, white peaches, nectarines, lemons, limes, or oranges

1 (1-liter) bottle plain or flavored sparkling water, chilled

mint sprigs

lime slices

Rhubarb Slush

This is fun way to celebrate with my girlfriends at our lake homes in the summer. You can cut down on the sugar, if desired, and use sugar-free gelatin.

In a large, heavy saucepan at medium-high heat, cook rhubarb, water, sugar, and lemon juice, stirring until smooth. Add strawberry gelatin and vodka. Let mixture cool. Place in plastic freezer bags and freeze for several hours or overnight.

Margaret Krouse - Administration

Serves 12

8 cups chopped rhubarb

8 cups water

3 cups sugar

½ cup lemon juice

1 small box strawberry gelatin

2 cups vodka

Pictured left to right:
Jenny, Scott and Chase Hoeppner
with Amy Ray, Ellen Chevillet,
John and Teddy Ray, and Maggie Byrne

Fall

In the fall, everything tastes better out of doors, surrounded
by the sights and smells of the season

Sunday Soup Dinner

Spiced Parmesan Cheese Crisps 114

Butternut Squash and Molasses Soup 104

Wildwood's Famous Chicken Tortilla Soup 109

Spinach Salad
with Hot Bacon Raspberry Vinaigrette 120

Pumpkin Cake Dessert 140

Outdoor Bonfire at the Lake

Warm Apple Cider

Frog Mix 111

Oven-Baked Caramel Corn 111

Lake Gage Chili 107

Picnic Loaf Sandwich 131

Applesauce Jumbles
with Browned Butter Glaze 133

Traditional Carrot Cake 142

Thanksgiving Dinner

CRANBERRY ORANGE CAPE COD 144

CRANBERRY SAUCE WITH APRICOTS AND RAISINS 119

PEAR, WALNUT, AND BLEU CHEESE SALAD 119

BRANDIED SWEET POTATOES 121

EGGPLANT AND HERB CASSEROLE 123

MAKE AHEAD MASHED POTATOES 125

SOUTHWESTERN-STYLE CORN BREAD DRESSING 126

GRILLED TURKEY WITH MUSHROOM GRAVY 129

JENNY'S PECAN PIE 136

PUMPKIN ROLL WITH TOFFEE CREAM FILLING
AND CARMEL SAUCE 141

Fireside Dinner

SYRAH

ROASTED RED PEPPER AND GOAT CHEESE PIZZA 113

FRENCH MUSHROOM SOUP 104

WINE LOVERS' SALAD 120

BROCCOLI WITH GOAT CHEESE 121

HORSERADISH RED POTATOES 123

FORGOTTEN ROAST 127

POACHED PEARS IN RED WINE 139

Beer Bread French Toast

The breakfast of champions! This is a hearty version of French toast.

This Beer Bread is also delicious toasted with jam, or served with a big hearty bowl of soup! The bread can be made up to 2 days in advance.

Beer Bread

Serves 6 to 8

3 cups self-rising flour

½ cup sugar

1 (12-ounce) can beer, room temperature

Heat oven to 375°. Lightly grease and flour a 5x9-inch bread pan. Mix together the flour, sugar, and beer. Pour into prepared pan, and bake for 55 minutes. Let rest in the pan for 10 minutes. Remove from the pan and cool on a rack.

French Toast

Serves 4

4 eggs

1 tablespoon milk

1 teaspoon vanilla extract

½ teaspoon cinnamon (optional)

Beer Bread (above)

Heat griddle and lightly grease. In a large bowl, whisk eggs, milk, vanilla, and cinnamon until well blended. Slice the Beer Bread into ¾-inch slices. Dip into the batter and cook until golden brown on both sides. Serve hot with your favorite syrup or fruit on top.

Michael Nelaborige - Friend

recipe hint

Real maple syrup is always a treat. Heating it up before serving takes it to another level. And it is out of this world with a little fresh-squeezed orange juice or melted butter added.

Italian Strata

An excellent breakfast casserole—especially since it is made the night before and refrigerated until ready to bake.

Brown the sausage in a skillet, stirring until crumbly. Drain the sausage, reserving the drippings. Sauté the zucchini, spinach, and onion in the reserved drippings in the skillet.

Combine the sausage, zucchini mixture, dry mustard, salt, pepper, cheddar cheese, Swiss cheese, milk, eggs, and bread in a large bowl and mix well. Cover and chill overnight in the refrigerator.

Preheat oven to 350°. Grease a 9x13-inch baking dish. Stir the mixture and spoon into the baking dish. Bake for 90 minutes or until light brown, watching carefully during the last 30 minutes as the strata tends to brown quickly.

Joyce Neubauer - Classic Steering Committee

Serves 6 to 8

1 ½ pounds mild Italian sausage, casings removed

1 pound zucchini, sliced

8 ounces fresh spinach, torn into bite-size pieces

1 onion, thinly sliced

1 teaspoon dry mustard

1 teaspoon salt

½ teaspoon freshly ground pepper

2 cups shredded cheddar cheese

2 cups shredded Swiss cheese

1 ½ cups milk

7 eggs

10 slices white bread, torn into bite-size pieces

Pumpkin Muffins

Heat oven to 350°. Line muffin tin with cupcake liners. Sift the flour, sugar, and cinnamon in a large bowl. Make a well in the middle and add the vanilla, butternut flavoring, oil, pumpkin, and eggs. Beat well. Stir in raisins if desired.

Pour into muffin tins, filling ⅔ full. Do not over-fill. Bake for 20 minutes or until a toothpick inserted in a muffin comes out clean.

Note: For a variation, top with chopped nuts.

Amber Whittington - Intern

Makes 16

3 cups self-rising flour

3 cups sugar

2 teaspoons cinnamon

1 teaspoon vanilla extract

1 teaspoon butternut flavoring

1 cup vegetable oil

2 cups canned or fresh pumpkin

4 eggs

1 ½ cups golden raisins (optional)

Serves 6 to 8

4 pounds butternut squash

4 (15-ounce) cans vegetable broth

1 cup water

½ teaspoon cayenne pepper

2 tablespoons butter

2 tablespoons molasses

1 green apple, thinly sliced (optional)

recipe hint

Whether you buy button, cup, flat, or cremini mushrooms, they are best fresh. Don't buy them more than three or four days before you plan to use them. To clean them, wipe with a moist paper towel. Don't submerge them in water, because fungi are absorbent and will get soft.

Serves 6

4 tablespoons unsalted butter

2 pounds mushrooms, sliced

½ teaspoon salt

1 teaspoon minced garlic

1 potato, peeled and diced

2 celery ribs

4 cups chicken stock

1 package Boursin cheese

1 ½ teaspoons fresh lemon juice

1 tablespoon chopped fresh chervil leaves

2 teaspoons salt

½ teaspoon freshly ground pepper

BUTTERNUT SQUASH AND MOLASSES SOUP

A bowl of warmth to add to your fall table.

Peel the squash. Cut in half and remove seeds. Cut into ¾-inch pieces.

Combine the squash, broth, water, and cayenne pepper in a large pot. Cook, covered, over medium heat for 20 minutes or until the squash is tender.

Purée the squash mixture 2 cups at a time in a blender. Return the blended soup to the large pot. Bring just to a boil and reduce heat. Simmer, uncovered, for 5 minutes. Add the butter and stir until melted.

Ladle the soup into bowls. Drizzle with molasses and garnish with green apples.

Anne Frantz - Merchandising

FRENCH MUSHROOM SOUP

Melt the butter in a large saucepan over medium heat. Add the mushrooms and salt and cook about 5 minutes. Add garlic and sauté for 2 minutes. Add the potato, celery, and chicken stock and bring to a boil. Reduce heat to low; cover and simmer until the potatoes are soft, about 30 minutes.

Purée the soup in batches in a food processor or blender. Return puréed soup to the saucepan and crumble in the cheese. Whisk until cheese is thoroughly melted. Stir in lemon juice, chervil, salt and pepper.

Serve immediately, or let cool to room temperature, cover and store in the refrigerator for up to 2 days.

Donna Watson - Maryland Sales Representative

butternut squash and molasses soup

lake gage chili

LAKE GAGE CHILI

This chili is a combination of many cooks and many recipes. It's a "killer white chili"!

Heat oil in a large heavy pot over medium-low heat. Add the onion and peppers. Cook, stirring occasionally, until soft, about 10 minutes. Add the garlic and cook 2 minutes longer.

Add the beans, salsa, tomatoes, corn, chicken broth, beer, and cumin. Simmer, uncovered, over medium heat for 20 minutes. Add cooked chicken, cover and simmer an additional 20 minutes. Add Monterey Pepper-Jack cheese and stir to blend. Season with salt and pepper. Serve with garnishes alongside.

The Marina at Lake Gage - Leslie and Tom Byrne, Owners

Serves 6

6 chicken breasts, cooked and diced

3 tablespoons olive oil
1 large onion, chopped
1 red bell pepper, seeded and chopped
1 mild chili pepper, seeded and chopped
2 cloves garlic, chopped
4 (15-ounce) cans Great Northern beans
1 (16-ounce) jar salsa
1 (14-ounce) can chopped tomatoes
1 (15-ounce) can yellow corn
2 cups chicken broth
1 (12-ounce) can or bottle of beer
1 teaspoon ground cumin
1 cup shredded Monterey Pepper-Jack cheese
salt and pepper to taste

fresh cilantro, for garnish
chopped red onion, for garnish

POTATO CHEESE SOUP

This is one cozy bowl of soup! Add slippers and a fire for a perfect winter supper.

Combine the potatoes, water, and salt in a saucepan. Cook for 20 minutes or until tender; do not drain. Heat the oil in a small skillet. Sauté the onion for 10 minutes or until translucent.

Purée the undrained potatoes and onion in a food processor or blender. Pour into a large saucepan. Cook over medium heat until heated through. Add milk to the desired consistency. Stir in the cheese, butter, pepper, garlic, and parsley. Cook until heated through.

Note: You may add 1 (10-ounce) package of frozen peas for a new twist.

Colleen Wegener - Marketing

Serves 4

4 cups peeled chopped potatoes
1½ cups water
2 teaspoons salt
1 tablespoon olive oil
1 onion, chopped

1¾ to 2 cups milk
1 cup shredded cheddar cheese
2 tablespoons butter
½ teaspoon pepper
⅛ teaspoon minced garlic
1 tablespoon parsley

Serves 6 to 8

2 pounds lean beef stew meat, cut into cubes

4 carrots, peeled and cut into chunks

3 large potatoes, peeled and cut into chunks

2 onions, peeled and quartered

3 cloves garlic, minced

3 teaspoons celery seeds

1 teaspoon thyme

2 teaspoons salt

2 teaspoons pepper

2 ½ cups V-8 juice

½ cup red wine

1 tablespoon Dijon mustard

2 tablespoons brown sugar

3 tablespoons tapioca

SLOW COOKED BEEF STEW

Because this stew bakes in the oven for five hours, it's a great dish to make on a cold, wintry Sunday. It makes the house smell wonderful!

Heat oven to 275°. In a very large bowl, combine the beef, carrots, potatoes, onions, garlic, celery seeds, thyme, salt and pepper and mix well. Set aside.

In a separate bowl, whisk together the V-8 juice, wine, mustard, brown sugar, and tapioca. Add mixture to the vegetables and stir well to blend. Transfer to a Dutch oven. Cover tightly and bake for 5 hours.

Patti Pine - Sales

WILDWOOD'S FAMOUS CHICKEN TORTILLA SOUP

The best thing about this soup, other than the taste, is that the only thing you have to cut up is the chicken.

Boil the chicken in enough water to cover in a large stockpot until cooked through. Drain the chicken, reserving 4 cups of broth. Cool the chicken slightly and shred.

In a stockpot, combine the chicken, reserved broth, tomatoes with green chilies, tomatoes, hominy, pinto beans, kidney beans, taco seasoning mix, and ranch salad dressing. Bring to a boil and reduce heat. Simmer for 30 minutes.

Ladle into soup bowls. Sprinkle with white tortilla chips and shredded Monterey Jack cheese.

Dana Manning - Friend

Serves 6

4 boneless skinless chicken breasts

3 (14-ounce) cans tomatoes with green chilies
1 (14-ounce) can diced tomatoes
1 (30-ounce) can white or golden hominy
1 (16-ounce) can pinto beans
1 (15-ounce) can dark red kidney beans
1 envelope taco seasoning mix
1 envelope ranch salad dressing mix

white tortilla chips
shredded Monterey Jack cheese

oven-baked caramel corn

FROG MIX

This recipe is from my favorite little bar in South Carolina. It's a British pub called The Frog & Brassiere. This snack mix recipe came from the owner.

Pour the oil into a large plastic food storage bag and shake to coat the sides evenly. Add the dressing mix and shake well. Add the Bugles, crackers, cereal, pretzels, and peanuts and shake to coat well. Store in a large airtight container.

Patti Reedy Parker - Granddaughter of Vera Bradley / North & South Carolina Sales Representative

Serves 10

1 bottle butter-flavor popcorn oil

1 envelope ranch salad dressing mix

1 (6-ounce) package Bugles

1 (10-ounce) package Cheez-It crackers

1 (12-ounce) package Rice Chex

1 (16-ounce) package Wheat Chex

1 (14-ounce) package pretzels (sticks, twists or rounds)

1 (12-ounce) can peanuts

OVEN-BAKED CARAMEL CORN

Fun for fall! Plus it fills the house with a toasty sweet smell as it bakes.

Heat oven to 225°. Mix butter, brown sugar, corn syrup, and cream of tartar in a sauce pan on the stove. Bring to a boil for 5 minutes, stirring continuously. Remove from heat. Stir in baking soda. Place popcorn in a large roaster pan, pour carmel mixture over popcorn, and stir.

Bake for 50 minutes, stirring every 10 minutes.

Peggy Gerardot - Friend

Makes 10 to 12 quarts

1 cup (2 sticks) butter

2 cups brown sugar

½ cup corn syrup

pinch of cream of tartar

1 teaspoon baking soda

10-12 quarts popcorn, popped

Pictured opposite:
John Ray, great-grandson of Vera Bradley,
with friend Annie Chevillet

ROASTED RED PEPPER AND GOAT CHEESE PIZZA

Pictured on page 145.

In a non-metal bowl, soak the sun-dried tomatoes in enough hot water to cover them until softened; drain and pat dry. If the tomatoes are packed in oil, you don't need to soak them.

Heat oven to 425°. With an electric mixer, beat the goat cheese and cream cheese in a small mixing bowl until smooth. Spread over pizza crust. Sprinkle with oregano, basil, and Italian seasoning. Layer the spinach, roasted peppers, sun-dried tomatoes, and artichoke hearts over the crust. Sprinkle the Parmesan cheese and feta cheese over the top.

Place on a pizza stone or round baking sheet. Bake for 15 to 20 minutes or until it is heated through and the bottom is crisp.

Cut into 1-inch pieces and serve as an appetizer, or serve with a lettuce salad as an entrée.

Stefanie Chevillet - Friend

Serves 6

10 sun-dried tomatoes

4 ounces goat cheese, softened
3 ounces cream cheese, softened

1 10-inch baked homemade pizza crust or purchased pizza crust

2 teaspoons oregano
2 teaspoons basil
2 teaspoons Italian seasoning
1 cup trimmed fresh spinach
1 (4-ounce) jar roasted red peppers, rinsed, chopped
1 (14-ounce) can artichoke hearts, drained, chopped

¾ cup grated Parmesan or Romano cheese
1 cup crumbled feta cheese

SOUTHERN VIDALIA ONION DIP

This is fast and easy, and tastes great! It's a fun dip for friends and family. You can make as much as you want—just use equal amounts of the onions, mayonnaise, and cheddar cheese.

Heat oven to 350°. Combine onion, mayonnaise, and cheese in a large bowl and mix well. Spoon into a baking dish and sprinkle with paprika. Bake until it bubbles, about 15 minutes. Brown top and let cool until serving. Great with tortilla chips, crackers, or vegetables.

Brigid Berry - Retailer (LA Bag Lady, Columbia, South Carolina)

Serves 8 to 10

2 cups chopped Vidalia onion
2 cups mayonnaise
2 cups shredded sharp cheddar cheese
paprika

Pictured opposite above left: John and Teddy Ray, great-grandsons of Vera Bradley; Ellen Chevillet; and granddaughter of Vera Bradley, Amy Ray

Pictured opposite bottom right: Teddy Ray

SOUTHWESTERN CORN BREAD

Serves 6

⅓ cup shortening

1 cup cornmeal

½ teaspoon salt

½ teaspoon baking soda

1 (10½-ounce) can cream-style corn

2 eggs, slightly beaten

⅝ cup buttermilk

1 (4-ounce) can green chilies, diced and drained

1 cup grated cheddar cheese

The best corn bread recipe we've tasted! Wonderful with fall soups or chili.

Heat oven to 375°. Lightly grease a 9-inch pie pan. Mix together the shortening, cornmeal, salt, soda, corn, eggs, and buttermilk until just moistened. Pour half of the mixture into the prepared pan. Top with chopped chilies and cheese, then cover with the remaining corn bread mixture. Bake for 35 to 40 minutes until browned on top and a toothpick inserted in the center comes out clean.

Lita Hegemier - Quality

SPICED PARMESAN CHEESE CRISPS

Makes 80 crisps

10 egg roll wrappers

2 large egg whites, lightly beaten

1 cup (4 ounces) grated fresh Parmesan cheese

1 teaspoon dried oregano

1 teaspoon dried basil

⅓ teaspoon cayenne pepper

About 15 minutes after you start this recipe, you can start munching on this crunchy snack—perhaps while watching movies.

Heat oven to 325°. Coat baking sheets with nonstick cooking spray. Place the egg roll wrappers in a single layer on baking sheets. Lightly brush with the egg whites, then cut each wrapper into 8 wedges. Combine the cheese, oregano, basil, and cayenne pepper in a bowl, then sprinkle evenly over the wedges. Bake for 5 minutes or until lightly browned.

Cheri Lantz - Sales

southwestern corn bread

Serves 4

1 large head romaine

1 garlic clove
½ cup salad oil
6 anchovy fillets, drained, chopped
1 ½ teaspoons Worcestershire sauce
¾ teaspoon salt
¼ teaspoon dry mustard
¼ teaspoon freshly ground pepper

1 egg
¼ cup crumbled bleu cheese
2 tablespoons grated Parmesan cheese
2 tablespoons lemon juice

1 cup Caesar salad croutons

CAESAR SALAD

The bleu cheese is a nice addition to this Caesar salad variation.

Trim the core from the lettuce and separate the leaves. Rinse under cold water and shake to drain. Pat dry with paper towels. Wrap in plastic wrap. Chill for several hours.

To make the dressing: Cut the garlic in half. Reserve 1 half of the garlic. Crush the remaining garlic. Combine the crushed garlic with the oil, anchovies, Worcestershire sauce, salt, dry mustard, and pepper in a jar with a tight-fitting lid. Cover and shake vigorously. Chill until serving time.

Rub the reserved garlic inside a wooden salad bowl; discard. Cut out the large ribs from the large leaves of the romaine. Tear the leaves into bite-size pieces and place in the prepared salad bowl.

When ready to serve, bring 2 inches of water to a boil in a small saucepan. Turn off heat. Lower the egg carefully into the water. Let stand for 1 minute; drain. Shake the dressing and pour over the romaine. Sprinkle with the bleu cheese and Parmesan cheese and toss to coat well. Break the egg over the center of the salad. Pour the lemon juice over the egg. Toss the salad to coat well. Sprinkle with the croutons and toss quickly. Serve immediately.

Sharon Keogh - Retailer (Monograms & More, Hinsdale, Illinois)

CALICO BAKED BEANS

A perfect colorful side dish to bring to a barbeque.

Heat oven to 350°. Combine the beans, onions, oil, brown sugar, and barbeque sauce in a bowl and mix well. Spoon into a 4-quart baking dish. Sprinkle with the bacon. Bake, covered, for 60 minutes. Uncover and bake for 30 minutes longer.

Kathy Reedy Ray - Granddaughter of Vera Bradley / Michigan Sales Representative

Serves 16

1 (16-ounce) can green beans, drained

1 (16-ounce) can wax beans, drained

1 (16-ounce) can red kidney beans, drained

1 (16-ounce) can lima beans, drained

1 (16-ounce) can baked beans in tomato sauce

1 (16-ounce) can white kidney beans, drained

2 medium onions, chopped

3 tablespoons olive oil

¼ to ⅓ cup packed brown sugar

1 (12-ounce) jar hickory barbeque sauce

4 slices bacon, cooked, crumbled (optional)

helpful hint

Beans and other legumes would be nearly a perfect food, full of protein, vitamins and fiber... if it wasn't for one little problem. You can cook them wrong and hurry your guests out the door, or you can cook them correctly. Here's how: When cooking dried beans, before soaking, boil the little trouble-makers for 10 minutes. Discard the water, refill your container with fresh water and let them soak overnight.

CRANBERRY SAUCE WITH APRICOTS AND RAISINS

This recipe has been brought back from our first cookbook. It's a holiday favorite.

Combine the cranberries, apricots, raisins, sugar, water, orange juice, and orange zest in a heavy saucepan. Cook over medium heat until the sugar dissolves, stirring constantly. Increase the heat to medium-high. Cover and bring to a boil. Boil for 8 minutes or until the cranberries pop, stirring occasionally.

Spoon into a serving bowl. Chill, covered, in the refrigerator. The sauce will thicken as it chills. You may prepare the sauce up to 4 days in advance.

Mary Beth Wahl - Friend

Serves 8

4 cups fresh cranberries

1 cup chopped dried apricots

1 cup golden raisins

¾ cup sugar

1 cup water

1 cup orange juice

1 tablespoon orange zest

PEAR, WALNUT, AND BLEU CHEESE SALAD

The flavors blend perfectly in this salad, making it a popular dish with almost any entrée.

Mash the garlic and salt in a bowl to form a paste. Add the vinegar, lemon juice, shallot, Dijon mustard, lemon zest, and black peppercorns and whisk well. Add the oil in a fine stream, whisking constantly. Set aside.

Arrange the lettuce on 6 individual salad plates. Divide the pears, walnuts, and bleu cheese equally among the plates. Drizzle with the vinaigrette. Serve immediately.

Susie Bruce - Friend

Serves 6

1 small garlic clove, minced

⅛ to ¼ teaspoon salt

⅓ cup red wine vinegar

1 teaspoon lemon juice

1 shallot, minced

1 teaspoon Dijon mustard

1 teaspoon lemon zest

2 teaspoons cracked black peppercorns

1 cup olive oil

1 ½ heads green leaf lettuce, torn into bite-size pieces

2 large pears, peeled, sliced

1 cup toasted walnut pieces

¾ cup crumbled bleu cheese

Spinach Salad with Hot Bacon Raspberry Vinaigrette

Serves 6

1 pound baby spinach, trimmed

1 cup thinly sliced fresh mushrooms

1 red onion, sliced, separated into rings

2 hard-cooked eggs, sliced

1 pound bacon, cut into small pieces

½ cup raspberry vinegar

¼ cup Dijon mustard

2 tablespoons sugar

¼ teaspoon Tabasco sauce or other hot sauce

½ cup olive oil

freshly ground pepper to taste

1 cup fresh raspberries

Gently combine the spinach, mushrooms, onion rings, and eggs in a large salad bowl.

Cook the bacon in a large skillet over medium-high heat until crisp. Drain the bacon, reserving 1 cup of the hot bacon drippings. Place the bacon on paper towels and pat dry. Crumble the bacon and add to the spinach mixture.

To make vinaigrette: Process the vinegar, Dijon mustard, sugar, and Tabasco sauce in a food processor. Add the reserved hot bacon drippings and oil separately in a fine stream, processing constantly. Adjust the seasonings to taste. Pour over the spinach mixture and toss to coat. Divide among 6 salad plates. Sprinkle with pepper and fresh raspberries.

Kim Colby - Product Development

Wine Lovers' Salad

Serves 6

½ cup olive oil

2 tablespoons red wine

1 ½ tablespoons red wine vinegar

1 tablespoon Dijon mustard

1 teaspoon salt

¾ teaspoon pepper

6 cups torn lettuce greens

1 cup shredded Swiss cheese

¾ cup chopped walnuts

This is a simple salad that is great for a family dinner or a larger event—just adjust the portions.

To make the vinaigrette: Combine the oil, wine, vinegar, Dijon mustard, salt and pepper in a salad cruet. Cover and shake vigorously.

Combine the lettuce greens, cheese, and walnuts in a salad bowl. Add the vinaigrette and toss to coat. Serve immediately.

Jill Nichols - Operations

Brandied Sweet Potatoes

Okay, this is what really got my boyfriend, Bill, to marry me.

Heat oven to 350°. Lightly grease a 7x11-inch baking dish. In a large stock pot, boil sweet potatoes for 45 minutes or until tender; drain. Cool slightly. Peel the sweet potatoes and place in a large mixing bowl; beat until mashed. Add the sugar, brandy, butter, salt, nutmeg, ginger, and pepper and beat well. Spoon into the baking dish. Brush with melted butter. Sprinkle with the orange zest and pecans. Bake for 25 to 30 minutes or until heated through. Garnish with orange slices.

Debra Bleeke - Customer Service

Serves 6 to 8

5 large sweet potatoes (approximately 4 ½ pounds)

¼ cup sugar

¼ to ⅓ cup brandy

3 tablespoons butter or margarine, melted

1 teaspoon salt

½ teaspoon nutmeg

½ teaspoon ginger

⅛ teaspoon pepper

1 tablespoon butter or margarine, melted

1 tablespoon orange zest

1 cup finely chopped pecans

1 orange, sliced

Broccoli with Goat Cheese

This is one of our family's absolute favorites! It's one of those culinary miracles where two pungent-smelling and strong-flavored ingredients marry into an exquisite dish. Serve over fettuccine or other medium-to-wide noodles or with medium-to-large pasta shells.

Melt the butter over moderate heat in a large skillet. Add the broccoli florets and toss them until thoroughly coated with butter and heated through, about 2 minutes.

Add the goat cheese and stir until it melts and coats the broccoli. Immediately pour the broccoli and cheese sauce over cooked pasta. Season with salt and plenty of black pepper.

Kim Colby - Product Development

Serves 4

¾ cup (1 ½ sticks) butter, cut into pieces

6 cups packed broccoli florets, parboiled until tender-crisp, about 30 seconds

1 pound creamy goat cheese, cut into pieces

cooked pasta

salt and pepper to taste

Eggplant and Herb Casserole

I learned about this dish when I lived in England. Over there they call it "Aubergine and Herb Casserole." The herbs really make this dish. Sometimes I make several of these in smaller baking dishes and freeze them.

Heat oven to 350°. To make the tomato sauce: Chop the tomatoes into small cubes. Heat the olive oil in a saucepan and sauté the onion and garlic, stirring frequently, for 1 minute. Add the chopped tomatoes, tomato purée, oregano, basil, and thyme. Stir well and bring to a simmer. Cover and cook over a very low heat for 30 minutes, stirring occasionally.

While the tomato sauce is cooking, dredge the slices of eggplant in flour and sauté them in olive oil in a large pan over moderate heat until lightly browned on both sides.

Season the tomato sauce with the salt and pepper. Pour a layer of sauce over the bottom of a 9x13-inch baking dish and cover with a layer of eggplant. Continue layering tomato sauce and eggplant, finishing with a layer of eggplant. Arrange the sliced mozzarella over the top. Bake for about 45 minutes.

Susan Giles - Sales

Serves 6 to 8

3½ pounds ripe plum tomatoes, skinned, or 2 (24-ounce) cans of plum tomatoes, drained

1 tablespoon olive oil

1 large onion, chopped

2 teaspoons chopped garlic

6 ounces tomato purée

1 tablespoon chopped fresh oregano

1 tablespoon chopped fresh basil

1 tablespoon chopped fresh thyme

1 two-pound eggplant, sliced diagonally into ¼-inch thick pieces

7 tablespoons olive oil

flour

sea salt to taste

freshly ground pepper to taste

8 ounces mozzarella cheese, sliced

Horseradish Red Potatoes

Great with prime rib!

Heat oven to 425°. With a vegetable peeler, peel a 1-inch stripe around each potato. Melt the butter and add the horseradish, salt and pepper. Toss the potatoes in the butter mixture to coat. Arrange the potatoes on a rack placed inside a baking pan.

Bake for 40 minutes or until the potatoes are fork tender.

Catherine Hill - Vera Bradley Foundation for Breast Cancer

Serves 6

2 pounds small red potatoes

¼ cup butter

2 tablespoons prepared horseradish

½ teaspoon salt

½ teaspoon pepper

James' Famous Mac and Cheese

Serves 12 to 16

2 pounds penne pasta

4 tablespoons butter

½ cup flour

4 cups half-and-half

1 cup whole milk

2 pounds sharp cheddar cheese, shredded

1 crusty French baguette (day old)

4 tablespoons butter

4 tablespoons olive oil

2 cloves fresh garlic, minced or pressed

salt and pepper to taste

This recipe was created from several sources, including favorite restaurants, recipes, and good old-fashioned trial and error. It is my kids' favorite and became famous in our little town of New Albany, Ohio, as a favorite dinner party item for the kids. The adults would always eat it too!

Heat oven to 350°. Boil water and cook the pasta until just tender, about 10 minutes; drain and rinse with cool water. Return cooked pasta to the pot; set aside.

In a large saucepan, melt butter and slowly add flour, cooking about 2 minutes (it will absorb and become dry). Slowly add half-and-half, stirring constantly with a whisk, then add the whole milk, stirring slowly to ensure the sauce stays smooth. This process will take 10 minutes or so.

Mix the cheese thoroughly with the pasta in the large pot. Add the white sauce to the pasta and continue to mix well. Transfer to two 9x13-inch oven-safe baking dishes. You can chill, covered, in the refrigerator at this point for up to 1 day.

If desired, add the following topping:

Put day-old baguette (must be very dry) into a food processor and process into crumbs. Melt the butter and olive oil in a large saucepan. Add garlic, salt and pepper. Add crumbs and coat them thoroughly, browning slightly.

Bake the mac and cheese (with or without topping) for about 20 to 30 minutes. Watch it closely and remove when it bubbles along the sides.

You can freeze any leftovers for the kids!

James Shimizu - Marketing

MAKE-AHEAD MASHED POTATOES

Perfect for Thanksgiving dinner when you have a thousand things on the stove. Just make ahead, pull out of the refrigerator and bake.

Heat oven to 350°. Butter a 9x13-inch baking dish. In a saucepan, cover the potatoes with water, and boil until tender; drain well. Mash until smooth. Add the cream cheese, sour cream, butter or margarine, onion salt, salt and pepper and beat until smooth and fluffy. Spoon into baking dish. Dot with additional butter. Bake for 30 minutes or until heated through.

Kim Colby - Product Development

Serves 8

5 pounds potatoes, peeled, quartered

6 ounces cream cheese, softened

1 cup sour cream

2 tablespoons butter or margarine

2 teaspoons onion salt

1 teaspoon salt

¼ teaspoon pepper

butter

MOM'S TRADITIONAL STUFFING

Heat oven to 350°. Heat the oil in a stockpot over medium-high heat. Add the onion, garlic, and celery. Sauté for 10 minutes or until tender. Add the mushrooms, pepper, salt, sage, celery salt, and thyme. Cook for 5 minutes. Add the bread cubes and mix well. Add enough of the broth to moisten to the desired consistency, stirring constantly.

Use dressing to stuff the cavity of a 20- to 21-pound turkey or spoon into a large greased baking dish. Bake for 30 to 40 minutes.

Becky Bennett - Product Development

Serves 15 or makes enough dressing for a 20-pound turkey

2 tablespoons olive oil

1 cup chopped yellow onion

2 garlic cloves, minced

1 cup chopped celery

1 ½ cups sliced mushrooms

2 tablespoons pepper

2 teaspoons salt

1 teaspoon sage

1 teaspoon celery salt

1 teaspoon thyme

4 loaves white bread, toasted, cubed

3 cups chicken broth (approximately)

Serves 8

2 (8-ounce) packages corn bread mix

2 to 3 teaspoons cumin seeds

1 tablespoon vegetable oil

¼ cup (½ stick) butter or margarine

2 cups finely chopped celery

½ cup chopped onion

½ cup chopped red bell pepper

½ cup chopped green bell pepper

1 (8-ounce) package herb-seasoned stuffing
   mix

2 (10-ounce) cans reduced-sodium chicken
   broth

2 ¼ cups water

2 eggs, lightly beaten

½ teaspoon salt

½ teaspoon cayenne pepper

SOUTHWESTERN-STYLE CORN BREAD DRESSING

This is a delicious southern dressing perfect at Thanksgiving for a little different taste.

Prepare the corn bread mix using the package directions. Let stand until cool. Crumble into a large bowl.

Sauté the cumin seeds with the oil in a small nonstick skillet over medium heat for 3 minutes or until fragrant and light brown. Let stand until cool, then crush.

Heat oven to 350°. Grease a 9x13-inch baking dish. Melt the butter in a skillet over medium heat. Add the celery, onion, and bell peppers. Sauté until tender. Stir into the crumbled corn bread. Add the crushed cumin, stuffing mix, broth, water, eggs, salt and cayenne pepper and mix well.

Spoon into baking dish. Bake for 75 minutes or until light brown.

Colleen Wegener - Marketing

helpful hint

The flavor of seeds can be strengthened by toasting them. Cook them in a skillet over medium-high heat for 2 or 3 minutes or until golden brown, or bake them in an oven at 350°. Stir occasionally and keep a careful eye out, as they burn easily.

CUMIN GRILLED PORK CHOPS

Warm and spicy. Great for a fall barbeque.

To make marinade: Whisk oil, soy sauce, Worcestershire sauce, garlic, cumin, brown sugar, salt and pepper together in a large glass measure. Place pork chops in a large casserole dish so they are lying flat without crowding. Pour marinade over pork chops and refrigerate for 4 to 6 hours.

Remove pork chops from refrigerator 1 hour before grilling. Prepare grill. Grill pork chops for 4 minutes, then flip and grill for another 3 minutes.

Amy Byrne Ray - Granddaughter of Vera Bradley

Serves 6

6 bone-in pork chops

½ cup vegetable oil
¼ cup soy sauce
¼ cup Worcestershire sauce
1 teaspoon minced garlic
1 teaspoon cumin
2 tablespoons brown sugar
salt and pepper to taste

FORGOTTEN ROAST

My mother, Vera, used to fix this dish when: 1) She didn't know what time dinner would be, 2) She would rather be playing 18 holes of golf, or 3) She would be working all day and entertaining that night. The secret is to keep the oven CLOSED at all times. She even put a sign on the oven door, since the aroma tempted people to open it for a "peek"!

Heat oven to 400°. Place the roast on a rack in a roasting pan. Sprinkle generously with the seasonings. Place in oven. Roast for 1 hour. Turn off the oven and let the roast remain in the oven all day. DO NOT OPEN THE OVEN DOOR!

45 minutes before you are ready to eat, parboil the potatoes and place them in the roasting pan with the roast. Turn the oven back on to 400° and bake for 30 minutes for medium-rare, or 45 minutes for medium.

Barbara Bradley Baekgaard - Founder and Co-owner

Serves 8

1 standing rib roast (8 to 9 pounds)
seasoned salt
pepper
8 potatoes, parboiled

Grilled Chicken Skewers with Red Pepper Pesto

Serves 4

1 (7-ounce) jar red peppers, drained
½ cup fresh cilantro leaves
6 tablespoons olive oil
3 tablespoons balsamic vinegar
1 small garlic clove, chopped
½ teaspoon dry mustard
½ teaspoon ground coriander
pinch of cinnamon
salt and pepper to taste

4 skinless boneless chicken breast halves
2 tablespoons olive oil
salt and pepper to taste

½ cup whole toasted almonds

We would serve this dish at Apparel Markets for buyers and we never had enough! At home we marinated the chicken in tequila and lime juice before grilling… even better!

For the pesto: purée red peppers, cilantro, olive oil, vinegar, garlic, dry mustard, coriander, and cinnamon in a food processor until finely chopped but not ground. Season with the salt and pepper. (Pesto can be made 2 days ahead.) Chill, covered, in the refrigerator. Let stand for 1 hour at room temperature before serving.

Cut the chicken into 1-inch pieces and thread onto skewers. Brush the chicken with the oil. Season with salt and pepper. Grill until cooked through, about 5 minutes per side. Arrange on a platter and serve with pesto, which has been sprinkled with the toasted almonds.

Note: The pesto is also great with pasta.

Betheny Campbell - Wisconsin Sales Representative

recipe hint

Before baking or grilling with wooden skewers, soak them in water for 30 minutes prior to use. Otherwise they will burn.

GRILLED TURKEY WITH MUSHROOM GRAVY

My husband Bryan and I call this "Mercury Turkey." The first time I grilled it, I left the meat thermometer in and put the grill lid on. The thermometer exploded and we had to throw the whole thing out. That same day, we bought a new grill with a built-in temperature gauge. Turkey #2 came out great.

Mix the rosemary, pepper, salt, thyme, and tarragon in a small bowl.

Remove the giblets and neck from the turkey. Pat the turkey dry inside and outside with paper towels. Spoon Mom's Traditional Stuffing into the cavity. Tie the legs loosely to hold the shape of the turkey. Brush with the oil. Rub with the spice mixture.

Place the turkey on a grill rack. Grill over medium coals for 3 hours or until a meat thermometer registers 170° to 180° and the juices run clear. Place on a large serving platter and tent with foil.

Serve with Mom's Traditional Stuffing and Mushroom Gravy.

Serves 15

1 ½ tablespoons rosemary

1 tablespoon pepper

2 teaspoons salt

1 ½ teaspoons thyme

1 ½ teaspoons tarragon

1 (20- to 21-pound) turkey

2 tablespoons vegetable oil

Mom's Traditional Stuffing (page 125)

Mushroom Gravy (below)

MUSHROOM GRAVY

Mix the flour and wine in a small bowl to form a smooth paste. Melt the butter in a large heavy saucepan over medium-high heat. Add the mushrooms and rosemary. Sauté for 3 minutes or until the mushrooms begin to soften.

Pour any juices from the turkey collected on the serving platter into a large glass measure. Add enough chicken broth to measure 5 cups. Add to the mushrooms. Whisk in the flour paste until smooth. Bring to a boil, stirring frequently. Cook for 10 minutes or until thickened and light brown. Stir in the milk, thyme, and tarragon. Season with salt and pepper.

Kathy Reedy Ray - Granddaughter of Vera Bradley / Michigan Sales Representative

½ cup flour

½ cup dry red wine

3 tablespoons butter

12 ounces fresh mushrooms, sliced

2 teaspoons rosemary

4 cups chicken broth (approximately)

⅓ cup milk

1 teaspoon thyme

1 teaspoon tarragon

salt and pepper to taste

picnic loaf sandwich

Picnic Loaf Sandwich

Great for outdoor events like picnics and tailgate parties. Hawaiian bread adds a great flavor!

Slice loaf in half horizontally. Remove 1 to 1 ½ inch of bread from the center of the loaf top. Layer the cold cuts and cheeses inside the loaf. Slice into wedges and enjoy! Experiment with different dressings to dress it up even more!

Joanie Byrne Hall - Granddaughter of Vera Bradley / Pennsylvania Sales Representative

Serves 6 to 8

1 large round loaf bread, such as Hawaiian or sourdough

2 to 4 types of assorted cold cuts, such as salami, ham, turkey, or roast beef

1 to 2 types of assorted sliced cheeses, such as Swiss, cheddar, or jalapeño-jack

lettuce (optional)

Tomato Pie

Perfect pizza. You can create your own combinations for added flavor and color.

Bake pie crust at 425° for 8 to 10 minutes. Remove from oven and reduce temperature to 375°. While hot, sprinkle mozzarella cheese on top and let cool.

Slice tomatoes and place on paper towels, then arrange tomatoes on cheese. Combine mozzarella cheese, mayonnaise, Parmesan cheese, pesto, and pepper in a bowl. Spread over tomato slices. Sprinkle with basil. Bake for 25 to 30 minutes.

Elizabeth Miller - Daughter-in-law of Patricia Miller

Serves 4

frozen pie crust
1 cup shredded mozzarella cheese

5 plum tomatoes (or 3 large ones)
½ cup mayonnaise
1 cup shredded mozzarella cheese
¼ cup shredded Parmesan cheese
2 tablespoons pesto
½ teaspoon pepper
3 tablespoons chopped fresh basil

applesauce jumbles

with browned butter glaze

APPLESAUCE JUMBLES WITH BROWNED BUTTER GLAZE

These cookies are an autumn tradition. The Browned Butter Glaze makes them amazing.

Heat oven 375°. With an electric mixer, beat the shortening and eggs in a mixing bowl until light and fluffy. Add the flour, brown sugar, salt, baking soda, cinnamon, cloves, vanilla, applesauce, and mix well. Stir in the raisins and nuts. Chill, covered, in the refrigerator if the dough is too soft.

Drop the dough by rounded teaspoonfuls about 2 inches apart on an ungreased cookie sheet. Bake for 10 minutes or until almost no indentation remains when touched. Cool on a wire rack. Spread with Browned Butter Glaze and top with chopped nuts.

BROWNED BUTTER GLAZE

Heat the butter in a saucepan over low heat until golden brown. Remove from heat. Add the confectioners' sugar and vanilla and mix well. Stir in enough of the hot water to form a smooth glaze consistency.

Susan Britton - Friend

Makes 5 dozen

½ cup shortening

2 eggs

2 ¾ cups flour

1 ½ cups brown sugar

1 teaspoon salt

½ teaspoon baking soda

1 teaspoon cinnamon

¼ teaspoon cloves

1 teaspoon vanilla extract

¾ cup applesauce

1 cup raisins

1 cup chopped nuts

Browned Butter Glaze (below)

½ cup chopped nuts

⅓ cup butter or margarine

2 cups confectioners' sugar

1 ½ teaspoons vanilla extract

2 to 4 tablespoons hot water

APPLE PIE DELUXE

Servings 6

1 9-inch unbaked pie shell, or
 favorite pie pastry recipe

6 to 7 Granny Smith apples, sliced

1 teaspoon lemon juice

⅔ cup sugar

1 ½ teaspoons cinnamon

2 to 3 tablespoons butter

½ cup (1 stick) butter, cold, cut in small
 pieces

½ cup brown sugar

1 cup flour

Our family owned an independent department store that had a restaurant in it called "The Chimney Corner." It was famous as a ladies' lunch spot after shopping or having their hair done. My mother made most of the pies from scratch—Apple Pie Deluxe was the best seller.

Heat oven to 400°. Line a pie plate with pastry. Toss the apple slices in lemon juice and arrange them in the pie plate—pile them high! Combine the sugar and cinnamon in a small bowl and mix well, then pour over the apples. Dot the top with butter.

Cut the butter, brown sugar, and flour together in a bowl until they have a crumbly texture. Cover the pie with the crumb mixture. Bake for 50 to 60 minutes. Serve warm with vanilla ice cream!

Carol Overland - Retailer (Wilkins & Olander, Sturgeon Bay, Wisconsin)

GG's Raisin-Filled Cookies

These are an old-fashioned classic.

With an electric mixer, cream together shortening or butter and sugar until light and fluffy. Add eggs and vanilla and mix until blended. In a separate bowl, sift together flour, baking soda, and salt. Add to the sugar mixture. Blend. Chill, covered, in the refrigerator for 2 hours.

While the dough is chilling, place the raisins in a saucepan and add water. Start to simmer. Add sugar and flour. Cook until mixture thickens. Add lemon juice. Cool. Add walnuts.

Preheat oven to 350°. Line cookie sheets with parchment. Divide the dough in half. With one half of the dough, roll out on floured surface and cut with round cookie cutters. Place cookies on a baking sheet. On each cookie, spoon 1½ teaspoons of the raisin filling, leaving a border of untouched dough. Roll out second half of the dough and cut with round cookie cutters. Top the raisin filling with another round piece of cookie dough, cutting an X into the top of each cookie to vent.

Bake for 9 to 12 minutes or until the edges are lightly browned. Cool on wire racks.

Peg Hattman - Friend

Makes 18 cookies

⅔ cup shortening or butter

½ cup sugar

2 eggs

1 teaspoon vanilla extract

2 cups flour

2 teaspoons baking soda

½ teaspoon salt

2 cups raisins

⅓ cup water

¼ cup sugar

1 ½ tablespoons flour

1 tablespoon lemon juice

½ cup chopped walnuts

recipe hint

Baking parchment is easy to use, helps cookies to cook uniformly, and makes clean-up easier.

Serves 6

1 cup white corn syrup

1 cup dark or golden brown sugar

⅓ teaspoon salt

⅓ cup butter, melted, cooled slightly

1 teaspoon vanilla extract

3 eggs, lightly beaten

1 ¼ cups whole pecans

9-inch unbaked pie shell

fresh whipped cream

JENNY'S PECAN PIE

I've made this recipe for Thanksgiving and Christmas for my family since 1974. Everyone loves it! Not only because it is from my home state of Kentucky, but also because it is delicious and easy! Don't think about the calories, just enjoy!

Heat oven to 350°. Combine syrup, sugar, salt, butter, and vanilla and mix well. Add eggs and mix well. This is easy to do by hand—no mixer necessary.

Pour the syrup mixture into a 9-inch unbaked pie shell. Sprinkle the pecans over the top. Bake for 45 to 50 minutes. (Center should move slightly when shaken.)

Serve with fresh whipped cream.

Jenny Hammons - Friend

recipe hint

Granulated sugar is flavored with molasses to make brown sugar. Dark brown and light brown sugar are different because of the amount of molasses used. Always firmly pack brown sugar when measuring unless instructed otherwise.

Mini Chocolate Soufflés

I prepare these ahead of time, then excuse myself from the dinner table to pop them in the oven. The aroma of warm chocolate takes over as dinner is winding to an end. Everyone is served an individual soufflé, which makes an elegant presentation!

Heat oven to 375°. Lightly butter eight 6-ounce ramekins. Dust them with confectioners' sugar and place them on a baking sheet.

Melt chocolate in microwave or double boiler, stirring occasionally, until smooth. Set aside. Melt the butter in a saucepan. Stir in flour and cook until thickened, about 1 to 2 minutes. Add milk and whisk until smooth and thick, about 3 minutes. Remove from heat. Add melted chocolate and whisk until smooth. Whisk in egg yolks, vanilla, and liqueur. Set aside.

With an electric beater, beat the egg whites and cream of tartar at medium speed until soft peaks form, about 1 minute. Gradually sprinkle sugar on top and beat on high speed until egg whites are stiff but not dry.

Fold ¼ of the egg whites into the chocolate mixture to lighten, then carefully fold in remaining egg whites. Spoon the mixture into ramekins, filling ¾ full. Chill, covered, in the refrigerator.

Bake for 15 minutes until puffed and slightly cracked. Dust with confectioners' sugar and serve immediately with fresh whipped cream. You can also garnish with fresh fruit or nuts.

Note: Instead of the almond-flavored liqueur, try using any flavor that goes with chocolate (which is just about anything).

Betheny Campbell - Wisconsin Sales Representative

Serves 8

butter
confectioners' sugar

8 ounces semisweet chocolate
1 tablespoon butter
1 tablespoon flour
½ cup milk
3 egg yolks
1 teaspoon vanilla extract
2 tablespoons almond-flavored liqueur

4 egg whites
⅛ teaspoon cream of tartar
¼ cup sugar

1 tablespoon confectioners' sugar
whipped cream

My Dad's Favorite Apple Crisp

Serves 10

5 pounds McIntosh apples

grated zest of 1 orange

grated zest of 1 lemon

2 tablespoons orange juice

2 tablespoons lemon juice

½ cup sugar

2 teaspoons cinnamon

1 ½ cups flour

¾ cup sugar

¾ cup brown sugar

pinch of kosher salt

1 cup oatmeal

1 cup (2 sticks) cold butter, sliced into thin squares

Heat oven to 350°. Grease a 9x13-inch baking dish with nonstick cooking spray. Peel, core and cut the apples into thin wedges. Combine the apples with the orange zest, lemon zest, orange juice, lemon juice, sugar, and cinnamon. Spoon into the baking dish.

For the topping, combine the flour, sugar, brown sugar, salt, oatmeal, and cold butter in the bowl of an electric mixer fitted with the paddle attachment. Pulse on low speed until the mixture is crumbly. Spoon over apple mixture.

Place the baking dish on a cookie sheet and bake for 50 to 60 minutes or until the top is brown and the apples are bubbly. Serve warm with vanilla ice cream.

Stefanie Chevillet - Friend

One Cup Cookies

Makes 4 dozen

3 ½ cups flour

1 teaspoon salt

1 teaspoon baking soda

1 teaspoon cream of tartar

1 cup (2 sticks) margarine

1 cup vegetable oil

1 cup sugar

1 cup brown sugar

1 egg

1 tablespoon vanilla extract

1 cup Rice Krispies

1 cup rolled oats

1 cup coconut

2 cups (12 ounces) chocolate chips

This is a recipe that takes the traditional chocolate chip cookie and adds an extra crunch and flavor. Somehow with the Rice Krispies and the oats we almost convince ourselves that this cookie is a healthy snack!

Heat oven to 350°. Line cookie sheets with parchment. Whisk together the flour, salt, baking soda, and cream of tartar. In a separate bowl, mix together the margarine, oil, sugar, brown sugar, egg, and vanilla. Add the flour mixture and blend. Add the Rice Krispies, oats, coconut, and chocolate chips.

Drop cookie dough by tablespoons onto a cookie sheet. Bake for 10 to 13 minutes.

Mary Ann Gray - Indiana Sales Representative

POACHED PEARS IN RED WINE

This dessert is elegant but easy, and makes a memorable presentation. The simplicity of it is especially perfect as the finale to a large dinner. Because of the deep red color, it is particularly nice for fall, winter, or holiday dinner parties.

Place the whole cloves and cinnamon stick in a small muslin bag, or tie them in cheesecloth. In a large, heavy saucepan, combine the wine, sugar, lemon zest, lemon juice, and the spice bag. Bring ingredients to a boil, then reduce and simmer until the sugar dissolves, about 5 minutes.

Peel the pears and cut the bottoms flat so they will stand upright, and core them from the bottom. Place pears in liquid and poach them over low heat, approximately 15 minutes, turning occasionally to coat. Cool the pears in the liquid, then remove them and discard the spice bag.

Over very low heat, cook the remaining liquid down to a syrupy consistency, stirring occasionally, about 45 minutes.

To serve, place one pear in the middle of each dessert plate and spoon the red wine reduction over each. For an elegant touch, garnish each pear with a dark chocolate leaf or flakes of edible gold leaf (available at most bakery or candy-making stores).

Michael Nelaborige - Friend

Serves 4

1 ½ cups dry red wine

1 cup sugar

1 2-inch strip of lemon zest (no pulp)

2 tablespoons lemon juice

4 whole cloves (or 4 cardamom pods)

1 2-inch cinnamon stick

4 firm large pears, such as Bosc

Serves 15

1 (2-layer) package pudding-recipe yellow
  cake mix

1 egg

½ cup (1 stick) butter, melted

1 (16-ounce) can pumpkin

½ cup brown sugar

¼ cup sugar

1 ½ tablespoons cinnamon

1 (5-ounce) can evaporated milk

½ cup sugar

¼ cup (½ stick) butter, softened

1 cup chopped pecans

PUMPKIN CAKE DESSERT

This recipe is best when made one day ahead.

Heat oven to 350°. Grease a 9x13-inch baking pan. Reserve 1 cup of the cake mix. Combine the remaining cake mix, egg, and butter in a mixing bowl and mix well. Spread over the bottom of the baking pan.

Beat the pumpkin, brown sugar, sugar, cinnamon, and evaporated milk in a mixing bowl. Pour into the prepared pan.

Mix the reserved cake mix and sugar in a bowl. Cut in butter until crumbly. Sprinkle over the pumpkin layer. Sprinkle with pecans. Bake for 1 hour. Let stand until cool. Chill, covered, in the refrigerator.

Vi MacMurdo - Friend

Pumpkin Roll
with Toffee Cream Filling
and Caramel Sauce

Serves 8 to 12

¾ cup flour
1 ½ teaspoons cinnamon
1 ¼ teaspoons ginger
¾ teaspoon allspice

6 egg yolks
⅓ cup sugar
⅓ cup brown sugar
⅔ cup canned solid-pack pumpkin

6 egg whites
⅛ teaspoon salt

confectioners' sugar

¼ cup English toffee pieces
Toffee Cream Filling (below)

1 ½ cups prepared caramel sauce, warmed
¼ cup English toffee pieces

Heat oven to 375°. Spray jelly roll pan with nonstick cooking spray. Sift the flour, cinnamon, ginger, and allspice into a small bowl. Set aside. Beat the egg yolks, sugar, and brown sugar in a large mixing bowl with an electric mixer for 3 minutes, or until very thick. Beat in the pumpkin at low speed. Add the flour mixture and beat until smooth.

With an electric mixer, beat the egg whites with the salt in a mixing bowl until stiff peaks form. Fold ⅓ at a time into the batter. Pour into jelly roll pan.

Bake for 15 minutes or until a tester inserted in the center comes out clean.

Place a smooth kitchen towel on a work surface. Dust generously with confectioners' sugar. Run a knife around the edges of the pan to loosen the cake. Invert the cake onto the towel. Fold the towel over 1 long side of the cake. Roll up the cake in the towel. Let stand seam side down for 1 hour or until cool.

Unroll the cake. Sprinkle with toffee pieces. Spread with Toffee Cream Filling. Roll up the cake loosely to enclose the filling, beginning at the long side and using the towel as an aid. Place seam side down on a cake plate. You may prepare 1 day ahead and chill, covered, in the refrigerator.

To serve, trim the ends of the cake roll on a slight diagonal. Sprinkle with confectioners' sugar. Spoon some of the warm caramel sauce over the top. Sprinkle with toffee pieces. Cut into slices 1 inch thick and place on individual dessert plates. Serve with the remaining caramel sauce.

Toffee Cream Filling

1 teaspoon unflavored gelatin
2 tablespoons dark rum

1 cup whipping cream, chilled
3 tablespoons confectioners' sugar
½ cup English toffee pieces

Sprinkle the gelatin over the rum in a small heavy saucepan. Let stand for 10 minutes or until softened. Cook over low heat until the gelatin dissolves, stirring constantly. Beat the whipping cream and confectioners' sugar in a mixing bowl until stiff peaks form. Beat in the gelatin mixture. Fold in the toffee pieces.

Stefanie Chevillet - Friend

Serves 16

2 cups flour

2 teaspoons baking soda

2 teaspoons cinnamon

1 teaspoon salt

2 cups sugar

1 ½ cups vegetable oil

2 teaspoons vanilla extract

4 eggs

3 cups shredded carrots

½ cup chopped walnuts

Cream Cheese Frosting (below)

8 ounces cream cheese, softened

½ cup (1 stick) butter or margarine,
  softened

1 teaspoon vanilla extract

2 cups confectioners' sugar

TRADITIONAL CARROT CAKE

This is a tried-and-true favorite.

Heat oven to 350°. Sift the flour, baking soda, cinnamon, and salt together. Combine the sugar, oil, vanilla, and half of the flour mixture in a bowl and whisk well. Add the remaining flour mixture alternately with the eggs and carrots, stirring well after each addition. Fold in the walnuts. Pour into a 10-cup nonstick tube or bundt pan.

Bake for 40 to 45 minutes or until a wooden pick inserted in the center comes out clean. Cool in the pan on a wire rack. Invert the cake onto a cake plate. Frost with Cream Cheese Frosting.

CREAM CHEESE FROSTING

Beat the cream cheese and butter in a mixing bowl until light and fluffy. Add the vanilla and confectioners' sugar and beat until smooth.

Joan Bradley Reedy - Daughter of Vera Bradley / South Carolina Sales Representative

traditional carrot cake

CRANBERRY ORANGE CAPE COD

If you're expecting a crowd, mix up a pitcher of this cocktail ahead of time and refrigerate. Pour over ice and garnish with lime wedges just before serving.

Mix cranberry juice, vodka, Grand Marnier, and lime juice in a large pitcher. Pour over ice and serve.

Stefanie Chevillet - Friend

Serves 10

5 cups cranberry juice
1 ½ cups vodka
1 ½ cups Grand Marnier
¾ cup lime juice

HOT CARAMEL BLISS

Serve with a good book, snuggly blanket, and a roaring fire. It doesn't get any better than this.

In a medium saucepan combine the cocoa, sugar, and water. Stir over medium heat until the sugar is dissolved. Remove from heat.

In a microwave-safe dish, combine the caramels and water. Microwave on high for 1 ½ minutes until melted, stirring several times. Set aside ⅛ cup of melted caramel for later.

Combine the caramel into the chocolate mixture. Stir until smooth over medium heat. Slowly add the milk, stirring constantly until blended and hot.

Pour into cups. Top with whipped cream. Drizzle the whipped cream with some of the extra caramel sauce or sprinkle with chocolate shavings.

Lori Britton - Friend

Serves 6 to 8

⅛ cup cocoa
⅓ cup sugar
⅓ cup water

½ package caramels, unwrapped
1 tablespoon water

6 cups milk

whipped cream
chocolate shavings (optional)

Roasted Red Pepper and Goat Cheese Pizza recipe on page 113

roasted red pepper and goat cheese pizza

Winter

New Year's. What are you waiting for?
Pull out the best china.
Open that special bottle you've been saving, and
toast to old friends and new!

Tree Trimming Party

Holiday Garnet Martini 197

Champagne Shrimp 157

Hot Pepper Jelly
with Cream Cheese and Crackers 160

Herb-Roasted Oven Potatoes 170

Tomato and Green Bean Risotto
with Feta Cheese 172

Vera's Glazed Pork Roast 178

Chocolate Candy Cane Cookies 183

Gingerbread Cookies 188

Mexican Wedding Cakes 192

Mocha Logs 193

Sugar Cookies 193

Christmas Breakfast

Coffee and Orange Juice

Cinnamon-Sugar Plum Cake 151
or
Raspberry Cream Cheese Coffee Cake 154

Fruit Salad with Ginger Syrup 168

Holiday Breakfast Casserole 155

Holiday Dinner

CABERNET SAUVIGNON OR CHARDONNAY

CHEESE TRIANGLES 157

PEPPERONI AND ASIAGO PINWHEELS 164

SOUTHWEST ROASTED RED PEPPER BISQUE 156

PEAR, WATERCRESS, AND ENDIVE SALAD
WITH SWEET GORGONZOLA 169

SWEET POTATO PECAN CASSEROLE 172

WILD RICE AND CRANBERRY DRESSING 173

ZUCCHINI CASSEROLE 173

APPLE CIDER BRINED TURKEY
WITH SAVORY HERB GRAVY 174

BOURBON CHOCOLATE PECAN CAKE 181

KEY LIME ZINGERS 191

New Year's Eve

CHAMPAGNE OR SPARKLING MOSCATO SPUMANTE

DATES WITH GOAT CHEESE AND BACON 159

HERB-CRUSTED PORK TENDERLOIN
WITH BAGUETTE ROUNDS 160

LAYERED CAVIAR APPETIZER 163

SESAME CHICKEN KABOBS 164

SHRIMP AND GRITS TARTS 165

SMOKY CHIPOTLE HUMMUS
WITH GARLIC BAGEL CHIPS 166

COCONUT-CHOCOLATE-ALMOND CHEESECAKE 184

GÂTEAU AU CHOCOLAT 186

WHITE CHOCOLATE
AND PEPPERMINT COOKIE BRITTLE 194

garnet martinis

BANANA-NUT CHOCOLATE CHIP BREAD

This recipe belongs to Caitlyn, my youngest daughter. She has loved to cook since she was two, concocting many recipes that we had to try to eat! This was one of her first successes, and she has been making it ever since.

Heat oven to 350°. Grease a 5x9-inch loaf pan. With an electric mixer, cream the butter and gradually add the sugar, beating well until light and fluffy. Add eggs, 1 at a time, beating well after each addition. Add bananas; mix until smooth.

Sift the flour, baking powder, baking soda, and salt in a separate bowl. Add the flour mixture to the butter mixture, stirring just enough to moisten. Fold in the walnuts and chocolate chips. Pour batter into the loaf pan. Bake for 60 to 70 minutes or until a toothpick inserted in center comes out clean. Cool in the pan for 10 minutes. Remove to wire rack to complete cooling.

Sophia McAlpin - Retailer (Angelic Accents, Plantation, Florida)

Makes 1 loaf

½ cup (1 stick) butter or margarine, softened

1 cup sugar

2 eggs

2 cups mashed ripe bananas

2 cups flour

1 teaspoon baking powder

1 teaspoon baking soda

½ teaspoon salt

½ cup chopped walnuts

½ cup semisweet chocolate chips

CINNAMON-SUGAR PLUM CAKE

You'll have visions of sugar plums dancing in your head after tasting this delicious take on a traditional Christmas treat.

Heat oven to 350°. Butter a 9-inch springform pan. Combine the flour, baking powder, and salt in a small bowl. In a separate bowl, beat butter until fluffy. Beat in sugar. Add eggs, 1 at a time, blending after each addition. Add lemon juice and lemon zest; blend well. Beat in flour mixture. Spread batter in prepared pan.

Press plum wedges halfway into the batter in concentric circles, spacing slightly apart. Mix sugar and cinnamon in a small bowl; sprinkle over plums. Bake until cake is browned on top and tester inserted into center comes out clean, about 50 minutes. Cut around cake; release pan sides. Serve warm or at room temperature. For an added treat, top with a dollop of whipped cream.

Holly Wagner - Customer Service

Serves 6 to 8

1 ¼ cups flour

1 teaspoon baking powder

¼ teaspoon salt

½ cup (1 stick) unsalted butter, softened

¾ cup sugar

2 eggs

1 tablespoon fresh lemon juice

1 teaspoon lemon zest

5 large plums, cut into 1 ½-inch wedges

1 ½ tablespoons sugar

¼ teaspoon cinnamon

Garnet Martini recipe on page 197

Makes 18 muffins

3 large oranges, reserve juice and 2 teaspoons of zest for glaze

¼ cup sugar

2 tablespoons water

5 tablespoons butter

2 cups flour

1 ¼ teaspoons baking powder

1 teaspoon baking soda

½ teaspoon salt

¼ cup sugar

2 eggs

¾ cup vanilla yogurt

¾ cup milk

Orange Glaze (below)

1 cup confectioners' sugar, sifted

2 tablespoons orange juice

2 teaspoons orange zest

pinch of salt

ORANGE YOGURT MUFFINS

Heat oven to 375°. Spray muffin tin with nonstick cooking spray. Finely grate the zest from oranges. You should have about ½ cup of zest. (Reserve 2 teaspoons of zest for the glaze.)

Combine the zest, sugar, and water in a small saucepan. Stir over medium heat for about 2 minutes, until the sugar dissolves. Add the butter and stir until melted, about 1 minute longer. Set aside.

In a medium bowl, combine the flour, baking powder, baking soda, salt, and sugar and mix well. Set aside. In a large bowl, whisk together the eggs, yogurt, milk, and the orange zest mixture until smooth. Add the dry ingredients and stir until just blended.

Spoon into muffin tins, filling each cup about ¾ full. Bake until a toothpick inserted in the center of a muffin comes out clean, 15 to 20 minutes. Cool for 3 minutes and then remove from pan. Pour a small amount of Orange Glaze over each muffin.

ORANGE GLAZE

Combine all ingredients and mix until smooth and well blended. If the glaze is too stiff, beat in a few more drops of juice. Refrigerate leftover glaze.

Patti Reedy Parker - Granddaughter of Vera Bradley / North & South Carolina Sales Representative

entertaining hint

When setting a buffet, use multiple levels to make a dramatic and appetizing presentation. Plates should be stacked at different heights. Food can be served on cake pedestals, tiered serving trays, and boxes placed under linens. Tall candles, short votives, flower bouquets, and fresh greenery can be tucked in between for additional color and interest.

vodka on ice with caviar

Raspberry Cream Cheese Coffee Cake

Serves 16

2 ¼ cups flour

¾ cup sugar

¾ cup (1 ½ sticks) butter or margarine

½ teaspoon baking powder

½ teaspoon baking soda

¼ teaspoon salt

¾ cup sour cream

1 egg

1 teaspoon almond extract

8 ounces cream cheese, softened

¼ cup sugar

1 egg

½ cup raspberry preserves

½ cup slivered almonds

This makes a lovely coffee cake for a holiday breakfast and has quickly become a favorite of all at Vera Bradley.

Heat oven to 350°. Grease and flour a 9-inch springform pan. Sift together the flour and sugar in a large bowl. Cut in the butter until crumbly. Reserve 1 cup of the crumb mixture. Add the baking powder, baking soda, salt, sour cream, egg, and almond extract to the remaining crumb mixture and mix well. Spread over the bottom, and 2 ½ inches up the side of the springform pan.

Combine the cream cheese, sugar, and egg in a mixing bowl and beat until smooth. Pour into the prepared pan. Spoon the preserves over the cream cheese layer. Mix the reserved crumb mixture and almonds in a bowl. Sprinkle over the layer of preserves.

Bake for 45 to 55 minutes or until the filling is set and the crust is a deep golden brown. Cool for 15 minutes. Remove the side of the pan. Serve warm or cool. Refrigerate any leftovers.

Debbie Wilson - Administration

Dad's Sausage Gravy

This recipe is always a pleaser on a cold winter morning or when you have a hungry crowd for a casual brunch. It's simple to prepare and satisfying for the family. The basic recipe has been passed down for three generations.

Brown the sausage and remove from pan. Reserve drippings. (Hint: For a finer texture, run the sausage through a food processor for about 6 on/off pulses.) In the same pan, measure 6 tablespoons of sausage drippings (if not available, may substitute butter to equal 6 tablespoons of fat). Stir the flour into the fat, forming a roux.

Cook the roux until it is slightly tan in color and becomes bubbly. Add the milk, stirring constantly until milk gravy thickens to desired consistency. Add salt and pepper and stir in the sausage.

Serve over biscuits or toast.

Aaron Feagler - Information Technology

Serves 10

2 pounds pork sausage (1 pound mild, 1 pound hot)

6 tablespoons fat (sausage drippings or butter)

6 tablespoons flour

4 cups milk

salt and pepper to taste

Holiday Breakfast Casserole

This has been a family favorite since I was a kid… when casseroles were everyone's favorite. We always have it during the holidays or anytime we have houseguests. Make it the night before!

Heat oven to 325°. Cut the crust off the bread and discard. Lay the bread in the bottom of a 9x13-inch baking dish. Cover with a layer of Canadian bacon, then a layer of cheese. Mix the eggs and milk in a separate bowl and pour over the top. Melt the butter, then toss with the cornflakes in a separate bowl. Sprinkle over the top. Bake for 60 minutes.

Joanie Byrne Hall - Granddaughter of Vera Bradley / Pennsylvania Sales Representative

Serves 12

12 slices white bread (the softer, the better)
Canadian bacon
shredded sharp cheddar cheese

6 eggs, beaten
3 cups milk

¼ cup (½ stick) butter
2 cups cornflakes

Southwest Roasted Red Pepper Bisque

Serves 4 to 6

⅓ cup finely chopped fresh cilantro

¼ cup reduced-fat sour cream

2 teaspoons milk

½ teaspoon salt

2 teaspoons olive oil

2 cups chopped onions

½ cup chopped carrots

1 ½ pounds red bell peppers, roasted, peeled, chopped (about 3 large)

1 tablespoon tomato paste

½ teaspoon cumin

¼ teaspoon chili powder

⅛ teaspoon cayenne pepper

2 garlic cloves, minced

¾ cup cooked long grain rice

½ cup water

2 (10-ounce) cans chicken broth

½ cup milk

¼ teaspoon salt

⅛ teaspoon pepper

Serve this very pretty soup around the holidays—especially when you have houseguests.

Combine the cilantro, sour cream, milk, and salt in a small bowl and mix well. Set aside.

Heat the oil in a Dutch oven over medium heat. Add the onions and carrots. Sauté until light brown. Stir in the roasted peppers, tomato paste, cumin, chili powder, cayenne pepper, and garlic. Cook for 5 minutes, stirring frequently. Stir in the rice, water, and broth. Bring to a boil. Cover partially and reduce heat. Simmer for 15 minutes.

Process in batches in a food processor until smooth. Return to the Dutch oven. Stir in milk, salt and pepper. Cook over medium heat until heated through; do not boil. Ladle into soup bowls and top with sour cream mixture.

Cheri Lantz - Sales

CHAMPAGNE SHRIMP

Murphy, Jeannine's daughter, serves this every holiday. It has become a family favorite and tradition. She usually triples the recipe.

Combine the shrimp, scallions, champagne, and salt in a skillet. Bring to a boil and reduce heat to medium. Simmer, covered, for 5 to 7 minutes. Remove the shrimp to a warm plate and tent with foil to keep warm.

Whisk the cream into the liquid in the skillet. Bring to a boil over high heat. Cook until the mixture is reduced to ⅔ cup, whisking constantly. Whisk in the butter 1 tablespoon at a time. Return the shrimp to the skillet. Sauté for 2 minutes or until heated through. Sprinkle with parsley.

Note: To serve as an entrée or on a buffet, ladle the shrimp and sauce over hot cooked rice.

Jeannine Wallace - Friend

Serves 4

2 pounds raw shrimp, peeled, deveined

4 scallions, minced

1 ⅓ cups champagne

½ teaspoon salt

½ cup heavy cream

½ cup (1 stick) butter

chopped fresh parsley

CHEESE TRIANGLES

Heat oven to 350°. Combine the Swiss cheese, Monterey Jack cheese, onion, parsley and dill. In a separate bowl, beat the eggs and add the baking powder. Add to cheese mixture.

Take 3 individual sheets of pastry dough and lay on flat surface. Cut each sheet vertically into 3 even sections. Work with only 3 pieces at a time. Cover remaining phyllo pastry with a damp cloth. Brush butter on each strip and sprinkle with bread crumbs.

Stack the 3 strips on top of each other. Place 1 tablespoon of filling on the end of the strip. Fold like an American flag, making a layered triangle shape. Brush with melted butter to seal edges. Bake for 25 minutes.

Joan Maxwell - Merchandising and Licensing

Makes 60 3-inch triangles

1 pound Swiss cheese, finely grated

1 pound Monterey Jack cheese, finely grated

½ cup minced green onion

½ cup minced fresh parsley

2 tablespoons minced fresh dill weed

6 eggs

2 teaspoons baking powder

1 ½ packages phyllo pastry sheets

2 cups (4 sticks) butter, melted

bread crumbs

new year's eve buffet

DATES WITH GOAT CHEESE AND BACON

Simple to make and a lovely appetizer for any festivity. Perfect with a sweet bubbly wine.

Heat oven to 375°. Cut the bacon strips in half, width-wise, to make 24 pieces. Warm for 1 minute in the microwave. Set aside. In a small frying pan, heat the olive oil. Add the bread crumbs and cook until lightly browned, about 2 minutes. Remove from heat and let cool.

Cut each date lengthwise with a small paring knife. Stuff each date with a rounded teaspoon of goat cheese. Sprinkle with bread crumbs. Carefully wrap one slice of bacon, one time, around the middle of the date. Use a toothpick to keep the bacon secured, keeping the goat cheese on top.

Place in a shallow baking dish and sprinkle the remaining crumbs on top. Bake for 10 to 15 minutes or until warmed through. Broil slightly for crisp bacon on the top, if desired. Serve warm.

Michael Nelaborige - Friend

Makes 24 appetizers

12 strips precooked bacon

1 ½ tablespoons olive oil

3 tablespoons fine dry bread crumbs

24 large dates (use large Medjool dates), pitted

¼ pound fresh soft goat cheese

entertaining hint

Making an ice bowl or cylinder is a beautiful way to keep beverage bottles chilled or seafood cold. For a beverage chiller, select two different sized cylindrical containers with flat bases – a 1½-inch size difference is recommended to make a thick enough cooler. Use metal, plastic, or tempered glass containers. For seafood, use bowls.

To suspend inner container over outer container: Cut four strips of heavy tape (electrical or duct) and apply about 2 inches of each strip inside the small container perpendicular to the rim, spacing evenly in "quarters." Place small container inside large container and, while keeping centered, stretch tape and attach to outer container to suspend.

Insert slices of fruit, herbs, flowers, or greens, berries, etc. in between containers, then fill with water (leave ½-inch at the rim for expansion as it freezes). Adjust decorations. Freeze solid. To release, remove tape, pour hot water into inner container and quickly remove. Release outer container by briefly dipping into a pan of hot water. Display on a rimmed tray using a folded linen napkin to absorb water as it melts.

Pictured:
Cecylia Daczuk (top left)
and Jane DeHaven (bottom right),
friends of Vera Bradley

HERB-CRUSTED PORK TENDERLOIN WITH BAGUETTE ROUNDS

An unusually hearty appetizer with an elegant presentation.

Serves 10

1 ½ pounds pork tenderloin

¾ cup bread crumbs

⅓ cup chopped fresh basil
(5 teaspoons dried)

3 tablespoons chopped fresh thyme
(3 teaspoons dried)

1 teaspoon kosher salt

2 teaspoons pepper

2 tablespoons chopped fresh parsley
(2 teaspoons dried)

1 baguette, sliced thinly

1 jar peach salsa or chutney

Heat oven to 425°. In a plastic zipper-lock bag, toss together the bread crumbs, basil, thyme, salt and pepper. Moisten the pork with water, place in bag with the bread crumbs and press onto the tenderloin. Remove from bag.

Place the meat on a rack in a roasting pan. Bake for 35 minutes or until a meat thermometer reads 160°.

Let the meat set before slicing. This can be served at room temperature. Cut the tenderloin into thin slices. Sprinkle with parsley.

To serve, place 1 slice of pork on a baguette round. Top with a teaspoon of peach salsa or chutney.

Stephanie Scheele - Marketing

HOT PEPPER JELLY WITH CREAM CHEESE AND CRACKERS

I've been making this for years with a close friend for Christmas gifts. We make ninety to a hundred jars every year. People want to get on our list!

Makes 6 half-pint jars

6 cups sugar

1 cup vinegar

½ cup vinegar

½ cup hot peppers, seeds and all

1 cup bell peppers, seeds removed

1 package Certo

cream cheese

Place the sugar and vinegar in boiler on medium heat. Put the additional vinegar, hot peppers, and bell peppers in a blender and purée for 2 minutes. Pour peppers into the sugar mixture and bring to a boil. Boil for 5 minutes, stirring constantly; set aside for 5 minutes.

Skim the top of the jelly and pour in the Certo. Stir, then let stand for 3 minutes. Pour into jars and seal. Serve over cream cheese with crackers.

Holly Crumpton - Alabama Sales Representative

Shrimp and Grits Tarts recipe on page 165

shrimp and grits tarts

layered caviar appetizer

LAYERED CAVIAR APPETIZER

A special treat! This recipe comes from Glenna's mother, Roberta May "Boots" Yott. It has been one of Glenna's family favorites for years.

Line a 3x5-inch pan or mold with parchment. Combine the eggs and butter in a small mixing bowl and mix well to form a paste. Chill, covered, in the refrigerator for 1 hour.

Blend the onion and sour cream together, and set aside.

To prepare the mold: Layer by pressing half of the egg paste into bottom of the mold. Layer with sour cream, then top with remainder of egg paste. Pack firmly into mold. Refrigerate for at least 2 hours. Unmold and top with the caviar.

Serve with crackers and vodka.

Glenna Reno - Michigan Sales Representative

Serves 8

4 hard-cooked eggs, finely chopped
½ cup (1 stick) butter, softened

½ cup sour cream
1 small green onion, finely chopped

1 (4-ounce) jar caviar

recipe hint

Not all caviar is created equal. If you dismiss caviar as gritty or too salty, it's possible that the type you tried wasn't the highest quality, because a good caviar—fresh, carefully stored, and served just right—has a wonderful flavor.

Fresh caviar is extremely perishable and must be refrigerated from the moment it's taken from the fish to the time it's eaten. Pasteurized caviar is roe that has been partially cooked, giving the eggs a slightly different texture and a longer shelf life. Pressed caviar is composed of damaged eggs and a combination of several different roes.

Store fresh caviar in the coldest part of the refrigerator at 26° to 36°. Once opened, it should be consumed within a week. You can store an unopened tin of fresh caviar for 2 to 3 weeks, while pasteurized caviar can last for 3 to 4 months before opening.

When serving, choose bowls and utensils made of nonreactive materials such as glass, plastic, or wood. Traditionally, caviar is served with tiny gold or mother-of-pearl spoons. Always avoid using easily oxidized metals, such as silver or inexpensive stainless steel, which will react with the caviar, giving it a metallic taste.

A final note: Caviar should not be cooked or it will toughen dramatically. If using it in a recipe, always add it toward the end of the preparation, or as a last-minute garnish.

Pepperoni and Asiago Pinwheels

Makes 5 dozen

½ cup grated Asiago cheese

¾ teaspoon thyme

¾ teaspoon oregano

¼ teaspoon pepper

1 sheet frozen puff pastry (half of a 17.3-ounce package), thawed

2 tablespoons honey-Dijon mustard

1 2-ounce package pepperoni (about 24 1½-inch slices)

1 large egg, beaten

Mix the Asiago cheese, thyme, oregano, and pepper in a medium bowl. Cut the puff pastry in half to form 2 rectangles. Spread 1 tablespoon of mustard over 1 puff pastry rectangle, leaving a 1-inch plain border at 1 long edge. Place half of the pepperoni in a single layer atop the mustard. Spoon half of the cheese mixture over the pepperoni. Brush the plain border with beaten egg.

Starting at the side opposite the plain border, roll up the pastry, sealing at the egg-coated edge. Transfer the pastry roll, seam side down, to a medium baking sheet. Repeat with the remaining pastry rectangle, layering mustard, pepperoni, cheese mixture, and egg. Chill the rolls, covered with plastic, in the refrigerator until firm, about 30 minutes, or wrap them and chill for up to 1 day.

Heat oven to 400°. Line 2 baking sheets with foil and lightly spray with nonstick cooking spray. Cut each pastry roll into about 30 ¼-inch thick rounds. Transfer pinwheels to prepared sheets. Bake until golden, about 15 minutes. Transfer to a platter and serve.

Leslie Byrne - Daughter-in-law of Barbara Bradley Baekgaard

Sesame Chicken Kabobs

Serves 6

6 boneless skinless chicken breasts

¼ cup plus 2 tablespoons teriyaki sauce

¼ cup soy sauce

3 tablespoons vegetable oil

2 tablespoons dark sesame oil

2 tablespoons sesame seeds

2 medium red bell peppers, cut into bite-size pieces

2 medium yellow bell peppers, cut into bite-size pieces

2 to 3 Vidalia onions, quartered

Try pre-soaking the skewers in teriyaki. It adds flavor and slows charring.

Cut the chicken into 1-inch pieces. Arrange in a shallow baking dish. Combine the teriyaki sauce, soy sauce, vegetable oil, sesame oil, and sesame seeds in a bowl and mix well. Pour over the chicken. Marinate, covered, in the refrigerator for at least 3 hours.

Prepare grill. Drain the chicken, reserving the marinade. Bring the reserved marinade to a boil in a small saucepan. Boil for 2 to 3 minutes, stirring constantly.

Thread the chicken alternately with the red and yellow bell peppers and onions onto skewers. Place on a grill rack. Grill over medium hot coals for 5 to 7 minutes or until the chicken juices run clear, turning and basting with the cooked marinade.

Nancy Pishney - Retailer (Creative Needle Arts, Ltd, Traverse City, Michigan)

Shrimp and Grits Tarts

I love shrimp and grits! Holidays are not the same without these treats. Pictured on page 161.

Heat oven to 350°. Lightly grease three 12-cup mini muffin pans. Combine the chicken broth, milk, butter or margarine, and white pepper in a large saucepan and bring to a boil over medium-high heat. Gradually whisk in the grits; return to a boil. Reduce heat and simmer, stirring occasionally, for 5 or 10 minutes or until thickened. Add the Parmesan cheese and whisk until melted and blended.

Spoon 1 rounded tablespoonful of grits-and-cheese mixture into each miniature muffin cup. Bake for 25 minutes or until lightly browned. Make an indentation in the center of the warm tarts using the back of a spoon. Let cool completely in pans.

Melt butter or margarine in a medium saucepan over medium-high heat; add ham, and sauté for 1 to 2 minutes. Sprinkle the flour evenly over the ham and cook, stirring frequently, 1 to 2 minutes or until lightly browned. Gradually add the chicken broth, stirring until smooth.

Reduce heat and cook, stirring frequently, 5 to 10 minutes or until thickened. Stir in the parsley and white wine Worcestershire sauce, and spoon evenly into the tarts. Top each with 1 shrimp.

Bake for 5 to 10 minutes or just until warm. Garnish with chopped parsley, if desired.

Kathy Reedy Ray - Granddaughter of Vera Bradley / Michigan Sales Representative

Makes 36 tarts

2 cups chicken broth

1 cup milk

2 tablespoons butter or margarine

½ teaspoon white pepper

1 cup uncooked coarse-ground or regular grits

⅔ cup shredded Parmesan cheese

2 tablespoons butter or margarine

⅔ cup diced smoked ham

3 tablespoons flour

1 ½ cups chicken broth

3 tablespoons chopped fresh parsley

¾ tablespoon white wine Worcestershire sauce

36 medium shrimp, peeled and cooked

chopped fresh parsley (optional)

SMOKY CHIPOTLE HUMMUS WITH GARLIC BAGEL CHIPS

Serves 20

2 (15-ounce) cans garbanzo beans (chickpeas), drained

½ cup water

¼ cup plus 2 tablespoons tahini (sesame seed paste)

3 tablespoons plus 2 teaspoons fresh lemon juice

2 tablespoons olive oil

2½ teaspoons minced canned chipotle chilies

1 large garlic clove, minced

1½ teaspoons ground cumin

1 (4-ounce) jar sliced pimientos in oil, drained

½ cup chopped fresh cilantro

salt and pepper to taste

2 (6-ounce) packages roasted-garlic bagel chips

If you don't have time to make your own hummus, buy some at the market or specialty foods store, and mix in chipotle chilies and cumin to taste.

Reserve 3 tablespoons garbanzo beans for garnish. Blend remaining garbanzo beans with water, tahini, lemon juice, olive oil, chipotle chilies, garlic, and cumin in a processor until smooth. Add pimientos and process, using on/off pulses, until pimientos are coarsely chopped.

Transfer hummus to a medium bowl. Stir in cilantro and season hummus with salt and pepper. Sprinkle with reserved garbanzo beans. Can be made 1 day ahead—cover and chill. Bring to room temperature before serving. Serve with bagel chips.

Laura Vorderman - Friend

Pear, Watercress, and Endive Salad with Sweet Gorgonzola recipe on page 169

pear, watercress, and endive salad with sweet gorgonzola

CHINESE COLESLAW

Serves 8

1 (3-ounce) package ramen noodles

1 tablespoon butter

1 (16-ounce) package coleslaw mix

1 to 2 green onions, sliced

½ cup sunflower seeds

½ cup almonds

¼ cup vegetable oil

3 tablespoons sugar

½ teaspoon salt

This recipe is so simple, it's a great way to introduce kids to salad! They'll love to make it.

Break the uncooked noodles into pieces and sauté in the butter in a skillet. Combine the coleslaw mix, green onions, sunflower seeds, almonds, and sautéed noodles in a large serving bowl and toss to mix.

Whisk the oil, sugar, and salt in a bowl. Pour over the coleslaw mixture and toss to coat. Chill, covered, for 45 minutes. Toss the coleslaw before serving.

Judy Wintin - Planning

FRUIT SALAD WITH GINGER SYRUP

Serves 10

2 pears, cored and diced

2 apples, cored and diced

2 oranges, peeled, segmented, and cut into bite-size pieces

1 large grapefruit, peeled, segmented, and cut into bite-size pieces

1 cup sweetened dried cranberries

1 cup walnut halves

Ginger Syrup (below)

In a large serving bowl, combine the pears, apples, oranges, and grapefruit. Sprinkle salad with the sweetened dried cranberries and walnuts. Pour just enough Ginger Syrup over the salad to coat all of the fruit, and gently toss. Serve immediately.

GINGER SYRUP

1 ½ cups water

1 cup sugar

1 cup thinly sliced fresh ginger, unpeeled

Bring the water, sugar, and ginger to boil in a 2-quart saucepan, stirring until sugar is dissolved. Simmer 10 minutes, stirring occasionally, then remove from heat and let steep 15 minutes. Pour syrup through a sieve into a bowl, discarding ginger. Chill, covered, in the refrigerator for at least 2 hours.

Jenny Lynn McGee - Licensing Associate - McGee Eyewear

Pear, Watercress, and Endive Salad with Sweet Gorgonzola

The bitterness of the endive and the sweetness of the cheese create a perfect balance in this salad. Pictured on page 167.

Combine the endive, watercress, and pears in a large salad bowl and toss to mix well.

Combine the vinegar, mustard, and parsley in a bowl. Add the oil in a fine stream, whisking constantly until blended. Pour over the salad mixture and toss to coat. Sprinkle with the cheese.

Michael Nelaborige - Friend

Serves 6

2 heads Belgian endive, julienned

2 bunches watercress, trimmed

2 pears, cored and chopped

¼ cup white wine vinegar

1 teaspoon prepared mustard

1 tablespoon minced fresh parsley

½ cup olive oil

4 ounces crumbled Gorgonzola cheese

Serves 4

3 medium onions, thinly sliced

¼ cup (½ stick) butter

½ green bell pepper, chopped

2 tablespoons chopped pimientos

1 cup shredded Swiss cheese

1 cup cracker crumbs

2 eggs, beaten

¾ cup half-and-half

1 teaspoon salt

½ teaspoon pepper

Serves 6 to 8

9 medium potatoes, cut into ½-inch slices
  (Yukon Gold are best)

2 tablespoons olive or canola oil

2 teaspoons sea salt

2 cloves garlic, finely minced

olive oil (in a mister)

10 fresh rosemary sprigs (about 3 inches
  long)

8 fresh sage sprigs (about 3 inches long
  with 4 to 5 leaves)

freshly ground pepper

2 small yellow onions, minced

CHEESY ONION CASSEROLE

A great side dish that really goes with everything.

Heat oven to 325°. Sauté the onions in the butter in a medium skillet for 7 minutes or until tender. Add the bell pepper. Sauté for 4 minutes. Remove from heat. Stir in the pimientos.

Layer the onion mixture, cheese, and cracker crumbs half at a time in a medium baking dish. Whisk the eggs, half-and-half, salt and pepper in a bowl. Pour over the top. Bake for 25 minutes.

Jeannine Wallace - Friend

HERB-ROASTED OVEN POTATOES

A crisp and fragrant side dish; fresh herb sprigs make this recipe less labor intensive and double as a pretty garnish.

Place an 18-inch large iron skillet in the oven (or two smaller skillets) and heat to 400°. In a large bowl, toss the potato slices with oil, sea salt, and garlic to coat. Lightly mist herbs with oil and set aside. Carefully remove the hot skillet from the oven and add the potatoes, keeping them in a single layer as much as possible. Make sure the skillet is hot so the potatoes sear immediately.

Bake for 15 minutes until potatoes are browned on one side. With a metal spatula, turn the potatoes over and sprinkle with pepper and onions. Tuck the herbs in amongst the potatoes and return to the oven to continue cooking for 15 to 20 minutes longer. Turn the potatoes and herbs occasionally, until lightly browned and cooked through. Serve the potatoes on a warmed platter with herbs tucked around them.

Note: Cutting the potatoes into slices rather than wedges allows more of the potato to come into contact with the skillet, thereby browning them more evenly.

Veronique Poudrier - Product Development

Pictured:
Cecylia Daczuk, Maureen and Mike Catalogna
friends of Vera Bradley

new year's eve

Sweet Potato Pecan Casserole

This is a family favorite every holiday season.

Heat oven to 350°. In a large bowl, combine the sweet potatoes, brown sugar, cinnamon, ginger, almond extract, salt, and eggs. Fold in the marshmallows. Spoon into a baking dish. Dot with butter and sprinkle with brown sugar and pecans. Bake for 45 minutes.

Elizabeth Miller - Daughter-in-law of Patricia Miller

Serves 4 to 6

3 cups cooked mashed sweet
   potatoes (fresh)

1 cup brown sugar

2 teaspoons cinnamon

2 teaspoons ginger

2 teaspoons almond extract

½ teaspoon salt

3 eggs, well beaten

1 cup miniature marshmallows

¼ cup (½ stick) butter

½ cup brown sugar

¾ cup chopped pecans

Tomato and Green Bean Risotto with Feta Cheese

In a non-metal, medium bowl, soak the sun-dried tomatoes in enough hot water to cover them until soft; drain. Cut into thin strips. Drain the beans, reserving the liquid. In a separate bowl, mix the reserved liquid with the wine and broth.

Heat the oil in a large skillet over medium heat. Add the onion and garlic. Sauté for 3 minutes. Add the rice. Cook for 1 minute, stirring constantly. Add the broth mixture 1 cup at a time, stirring constantly, until each portion of the broth mixture is absorbed; this will take about 20 minutes. Add the tomatoes, green beans, basil, and salt. Cook for 2 minutes, stirring constantly. Remove from heat. Stir in the cheese. Serve immediately.

Stefanie Chevillet - Friend

Serves 6 to 8

8 sun-dried tomatoes

1 (14-ounce) can French-cut green beans

⅔ cup dry white wine

3 (10-ounce) cans chicken broth

2 teaspoons olive oil

1 cup chopped onion

2 garlic cloves, minced

1 ½ cups uncooked short grain white rice

1 teaspoon basil

⅛ teaspoon salt

¾ cup crumbled feta cheese

Wild Rice and Cranberry Dressing

Bring the broth and water to a boil in a heavy saucepan. Add the wild rice and stir gently. Return to a gentle boil and stir. Reduce heat and simmer, covered, for 50 to 60 minutes or until the kernels just puff open. Uncover and fluff with a fork. Remove from heat and let rest for 5 minutes. Drain off any excess liquid.

While your rice is resting, sauté the onions, garlic, and mushrooms in the olive oil over medium heat until tender. Remove from heat and toss in the pecans and cranberries.

Add this mixture to the cooked wild rice. Sprinkle with salt and pepper. Stir to blend all of the ingredients.

Note: This is wonderful if made the day before so all the flavors blend. To reheat, place the rice mixture into a lightly buttered casserole dish. Add ⅛ cup water and bake, covered, in a 350° oven until hot, approximately 40 minutes. It also freezes wonderfully. Thaw before reheating.

Colleen Wegener - Marketing

Serves 6 to 8

2 cups chicken broth

1 cup water

1 cup long grain wild rice, rinsed

1 medium onion, chopped

1 garlic clove, chopped

8 ounces mushrooms, sliced

1 tablespoon olive oil

½ cup chopped toasted pecans

½ cup dried cranberries

salt and pepper to taste

Zucchini Casserole

It's great to have a unique and delicious side dish everyone likes.

Heat oven to 350°. Combine the zucchini, Bisquick, vegetable oil, cheese, garlic powder, and eggs in a large bowl and mix well. Pour into a 9x13-inch baking dish and sprinkle Parmesan cheese on top. Bake for 50 to 60 minutes.

Note: Yellow squash is also delicious in this recipe.

Kim Colby - Product Development

Serves 4 to 6

4 cups grated or thinly sliced zucchini

1 cup Bisquick

⅓ cup vegetable oil

½ cup grated cheese (I have used Swiss and mozzarella)

½ teaspoon garlic powder

4 eggs, beaten

Parmesan cheese

Apple Cider Brined Turkey with Savory Herb Gravy

Serves 12

8 cups apple cider

⅓ cup kosher salt

⅔ cup sugar

1 tablespoon black peppercorns, coarsely crushed

1 tablespoon whole allspice, coarsely crushed

8 (⅛-inch thick) slices peeled fresh ginger

6 whole cloves

2 bay leaves

1 (12-pound) turkey

2 oranges, quartered

6 cups ice

2 turkey oven bags

4 garlic cloves

4 sage leaves

4 thyme sprigs

4 parsley sprigs

1 onion, quartered

1 (14-ounce) can fat-free, low-sodium chicken broth

1 tablespoon unsalted butter, melted

½ teaspoon freshly ground pepper

¼ teaspoon salt

1 tablespoon unsalted butter, melted

¼ teaspoon salt

½ teaspoon freshly ground pepper

Savory Herb Gravy (on following page)

This recipe makes an incredibly moist and flavorful holiday bird, and is sure to receive high praise. Better yet, cooking time is less than two hours.

To prepare the brine: Combine the apple cider, salt, sugar, peppercorns, allspice, ginger, cloves, and bay leaves in a large saucepan and bring them to a boil. Cook 5 minutes or until the sugar and salt dissolve. Cool completely.

Remove the giblets and neck from the turkey; reserve for Savory Herb Gravy. Rinse the turkey with cold water and pat dry. Trim excess fat. Stuff the body cavity with orange quarters. Place a turkey-sized oven bag inside a second bag to form a double thickness. Place the bags in a large stockpot. Place the turkey inside the inner bag. Add the cider mixture and ice. Secure the bag with several twist ties. Refrigerate for 12 to 24 hours, turning occasionally.

Heat oven to 500°. Remove the turkey from the bags and discard the brine, orange quarters, and bags. Rinse the turkey with cold water and pat dry. Lift the wing tips up and over the back and tuck them under the turkey. Tie the legs together with kitchen string. Place the garlic, sage, thyme, parsley, onion, and broth in the bottom of the roasting pan. Place a roasting rack in the pan. Arrange the turkey, breast side down, on the roasting rack. Brush the turkey back with butter and sprinkle with pepper and salt. Bake 30 minutes.

Remove the turkey from the oven. Reduce oven temperature to 350°. Carefully turn the turkey over (breast side up) using tongs. Brush turkey breast with butter, salt and pepper. Bake for 1 hour and 15 minutes or until a thermometer inserted into the meaty part of the the thigh registers 170° (make sure not to touch the bone). Shield the turkey with foil if it browns too quickly.

Remove the turkey from the oven and let stand for 20 minutes. Reserve the pan drippings for Savory Herb Gravy. Discard skin before serving. Serve with the gravy.

Savory Herb Gravy

Some of the steps in this recipe can be completed a day in advance; just cover and refrigerate. Finish the last few steps while the turkey cools before being served. It's a good idea to double or triple this.

Heat the oil in a large saucepan over medium-high heat. Add the turkey neck and giblets and cook for 5 minutes, browning on all sides. Add the water, peppercorns, parsley, thyme, onion, carrot, celery, and bay leaf and bring to a boil. Reduce heat and simmer until liquid is reduced to about 2 ½ cups (about 1 hour).

Strain through a colander over a bowl, reserving the cooking liquid and turkey neck. Discard remaining solids. Skim fat from surface, and discard. Remove the meat from the neck and finely chop. Add neck meat to cooking liquid and discard the bone.

Strain the reserved turkey drippings through a colander over a shallow bowl and discard the solids. Place the strained drippings in the freezer for 20 minutes. Skim the fat from the surface and discard.

Place the flour in a medium saucepan, and add ¼ cup of the cooking liquid, stirring with a whisk until smooth. Add the remaining cooking liquid, turkey drippings, salt and pepper. Bring the gravy to a boil, stirring frequently. Reduce heat and simmer 5 minutes or until slightly thickened.

Catherine Hill - Vera Bradley Foundation for Breast Cancer

Serves 12

2 teaspoons vegetable oil

reserved turkey neck and giblets

4 cups water

6 black peppercorns

4 parsley sprigs

2 thyme sprigs

1 yellow onion, quartered

1 carrot, cut into 2-inch pieces

1 celery stalk, cut into 2-inch pieces

1 bay leaf

reserved turkey drippings

3 tablespoons flour

½ teaspoon salt

¼ teaspoon freshly ground pepper

helpful hint

We all buy fresh herbs, then only use a few sprigs. Try immersing the leftover herbs in light olive oil. Make sure the herbs remain beneath the surface or they may spoil. No need to refrigerate. The oil will take on the flavor of the herb. This is a delicious way to add flavor to a sauté or dipping oil.

brandy glazed ham

BRANDY GLAZED HAM

This wonderful ham has been a holiday tradition for many, many years. Being from the South, we always have cheese grits and deviled eggs to go with it! We double or triple the glaze for dipping.

Place ham in a large heavy pot or Dutch oven with a cover. Cover the meat at least halfway with the equal portions of wine and water. Bring the liquids to a boil; reduce heat. Simmer for 2 hours, turning ham after 1 hour to cover the other side with the liquid.

While the ham is simmering, combine the mustard, cloves, cinnamon, ginger, nutmeg, pepper, jelly, scotch, brandy, and brown sugar in a saucepan. Heat until thickened, stirring well to blend.

Heat oven to 325°. Remove the ham from the pot and trim off all but ¼ inch of fat. Score the ham well with a knife and place it on a rack in a roasting pan with the scored side up. Cover with ⅓ of the glaze.

Bake for 1 hour, basting twice with the remaining glaze. Let the ham stand for approximately 30 minutes before slicing.

Linda Cuzick - Washington Sales Representative

Serves 16

1 (10- to 12-pound) smoked ham, bone-in

6 cups dry red wine

6 cups water

2 tablespoons Dijon mustard

¾ teaspoon cloves

¼ teaspoon cinnamon

¼ teaspoon ginger

¼ teaspoon nutmeg

¼ teaspoon pepper

3 ounces red currant jelly

¼ cup scotch

¼ cup brandy

½ cup brown sugar

GRILLED LAMB CHOPS

Serves 4

½ cup tamari soy sauce (low-sodium soy sauce can be substituted)

½ cup canola oil

1 small onion, chopped

4 garlic cloves, chopped

1 tablespoon basil

2 teaspoons rosemary

1 teaspoon thyme

½ teaspoon pepper

8 lamb chops

Whisk together the tamari soy sauce, oil, onion, garlic, basil, rosemary, thyme, and pepper until well blended.

Place the lamb chops in a non-metal dish. Cover with the marinade. Cover and place in the refrigerator for 3 or more hours. Occasionally, turn the lamb chops in the marinade.

Preheat grill. Remove the chops from the marinade and grill for 4 minutes on each side for medium-rare chops.

Joan Maxwell - Merchandising and Licensing

VERA'S GLAZED PORK ROAST

Serves 8

1 (5 to 6 pound) rolled boneless pork roast

1 teaspoon chili powder

½ teaspoon garlic powder

½ teaspoon salt

1 cup ketchup

1 cup apple jelly

2 tablespoons vinegar

This was one of Vera's favorite recipes.

Heat oven to 400°. Mix the chili powder, garlic powder and salt in a small bowl. Rub the pork with the seasoning mix. Place the pork on a rack in a roasting pan. Roast in oven for 10 minutes. Reduce the oven temperature to 350°. Roast for 35 minutes per pound, or until a meat thermometer inserted in the thickest portion registers 170°.

Whisk the ketchup, jelly, and vinegar in a saucepan. Baste the pork with the sauce approximately 15 minutes before the pork is cooked through. Bring the remaining sauce to a boil. Boil for 2 to 3 minutes, stirring constantly. Serve with the pork.

Barbara Bradley Baekgaard - Founder and Co-owner

holiday dinner

ANGEL PIE

Serves 6 to 8

4 egg whites
½ teaspoon cream of tartar
1 cup sugar

3 egg yolks
½ cup sugar
2 tablespoons water
3 tablespoons fresh lemon juice
1 tablespoon lemon zest

1 cup heavy whipping cream

This was one of my mother's favorite recipes and has been shared with many of my family members and friends. It was our Christmas Eve dessert for as long as I can remember and I still fix it for my family. Friends have also told me that they prepare it on that day.

Heat oven to 350°. Grease a 9-inch pie plate. In a small bowl, beat the egg whites until frothy. Pour into a saucepan, add the cream of tartar, and bring it to a boil. Add the sugar gradually and boil until stiff and glassy. Pour into the pie plate and bake the meringue for 20 minutes. Cool completely.

In a medium bowl, beat the egg yolks and gradually add the sugar, beating until creamy. Add the water, lemon juice and lemon zest. Cook the custard in a double-boiler until thick, stirring frequently. Cool completely.

In a mixing bowl, whip the cream until soft peaks form. Spread half of the whipped cream over the cooled meringue, then spread the cooled custard mixture on top of the cream layer. Finally, spread the rest of the whipped cream over the custard layer. Chill and enjoy!

Kathleen Piper - Retailer (Kirlin's Hallmark, Appleton, Wisconsin)

recipe hint

Egg whites should be at room temperature before they are beaten. A copper bowl is best for beating eggs, but if you don't have a copper bowl handy, add a pinch of cream of tartar when they have been beaten to the foamy stage. It adds just enough acid to add volume and stability. Beaten eggs are considered stiff enough if they do not slide when the bowl is turned on its side.

Bourbon Chocolate Pecan Cake

I've heard it said, "Forget falling in love. Falling in chocolate is much nicer." This cake would qualify.

Heat oven to 350°. Spread the pecans on a baking sheet. Bake for 10 minutes or until toasted and fragrant. Remove from the oven and cool. Chop the pecans coarsely.

Cut a circle of parchment to fit the bottom of a 9-inch round cake pan. Butter the cake pan well and line with the parchment, making sure it lies flat.

Melt the butter and chocolate in a double boiler over simmering water, stirring frequently. Let stand until cool.

Combine the sugar, baking cocoa and eggs in a large bowl and mix well. Stir in the melted chocolate. Stir in 1½ cups of the pecans. Stir in the bourbon.

Pour the batter into the prepared cake pan. Place the cake pan inside a larger pan. Pour enough hot water into the larger pan to come 1 inch up the side of the smaller pan. Bake for 45 minutes or until the cake is firm to the touch. The surface may crack a little. Cool the cake on a wire rack. Remove the cake from the pan, leaving the parchment attached. Wrap in plastic wrap. Chill for 8 to 12 hours.

Unwrap the cake. Invert onto a wire rack over a sheet of waxed paper. Peel off the parchment. Drizzle spoonfuls of Chocolate Glaze along the edge of the cake so that it drips down and coats the side. Spoon Chocolate Glaze over the top of the cake and smooth with a rubber spatula. Cover the side of the cake with remaining chopped pecans by pressing gently against the side. Chill, covered, until 30 minutes before serving.

Serves 12

2 cups pecan halves

1 cup (2 sticks) unsalted butter
8 ounces bittersweet or semisweet chocolate

1 ½ cups sugar
1 cup baking cocoa
6 eggs
⅓ cup bourbon

Chocolate Glaze (below)

Chocolate Glaze

Melt the chocolate and butter in a double boiler over simmering water, stirring until smooth. Remove from heat. Cool for 5 minutes.

4 ounces bittersweet or semisweet chocolate
½ cup (1 stick) unsalted butter

Debbie Peterson - Vera Bradley Classic Steering Committee

chocolate candy cane cookies

Chocolate Candy Cane Cookies

For the cookies, whisk the flour, cocoa, and salt in a medium bowl to blend. With an electric mixer, beat the sugar and butter in a large bowl until well blended. Beat in the egg. Add the dry ingredients; beat until blended. Chill, covered, in the refrigerator for 1 hour.

Preheat oven to 350°. Line 2 baking sheets with parchment. Scoop out dough by level tablespoonfuls, then roll into smooth balls. Place balls on prepared baking sheets, spacing about 2 inches apart. Using your hand or the bottom of a glass, flatten each ball to a 2-inch-round (edges will crack).

Bake until cookies no longer look wet and a small indentation appears when tops of cookies are lightly touched with fingers, about 11 minutes. Do not over-bake or cookies will become too crisp. Cool on sheet about 5 minutes. Transfer cookies to a rack and cool completely.

For the filling, use an electric mixer to beat confectioners' sugar and butter in a medium bowl until well blended. Add the peppermint extract and food coloring. Beat until light pink and well blended, adding more food coloring by drops if darker pink color is desired.

Spread 2 generous teaspoons of the filling evenly over flat side of a cookie to the edges; top with another cookie, flat side down, pressing gently to adhere. Repeat with remaining cookies and peppermint filling.

Place crushed candy canes on a plate. Roll edges of cookie sandwiches in crushed candies (candies will adhere to filling). Store in a single layer in an airtight container at room temperature for up to 3 days or freeze for up to 2 weeks.

Renee Long - Marketing

Makes 18 sandwich cookies

1 ¾ cups flour

½ cup unsweetened cocoa powder (preferably Dutch-processed)

¼ teaspoon salt

1 cup sugar

¾ cup (1 ½ sticks) unsalted butter, softened

1 large egg

1 cup plus 2 tablespoons confectioners' sugar

¾ cup (1 ½ sticks) unsalted butter, softened

¾ teaspoon peppermint extract

2 drops (or more) red food coloring

½ cup crushed red-and-white-striped candy canes or hard peppermint candies (about 4 ounces)

Serves 10 to 12

1 ½ cups chocolate wafer cookie crumbs
  (28 to 30 cookies)

3 tablespoons sugar

¼ cup (½ stick) butter or margarine, melted

4 (8-ounce) packages cream cheese,
  softened

3 large eggs

1 cup sugar

1 (6-ounce) package flaked coconut

1 (11.5-ounce) package milk chocolate
  morsels

½ cup slivered almonds, toasted

1 teaspoon vanilla extract

½ cup semisweet chocolate morsels

toasted chopped almonds (optional)

COCONUT-CHOCOLATE-ALMOND CHEESECAKE

Tempting and decadent!

Heat oven to 350°. Stir together the cookie crumbs, sugar, and melted butter or margarine, then press into the bottom of a 10-inch springform pan. Bake for 8 minutes. Cool.

With an electric mixer, beat the softened cream cheese for 2 minutes. Add eggs and sugar; beat at medium speed until smooth. Stir in the coconut, milk chocolate morsels, almonds, and vanilla. Pour into pan. Bake for 1 hour. Cool on a wire rack.

On stove top, melt chocolate morsels in a double-boiler. Using a teaspoon, drizzle melted chocolate in a circular pattern over the top of the cheesecake. Cover and chill for 8 hours. Can be chilled for up to 5 days.

Garnish with toasted chopped almonds, if desired.

Stephanie Scheele - Marketing

recipe hint

To prevent a cheesecake from cracking, you could bake it in a water bath. Use foil to wrap the springform pan, pulling it tightly to prevent water getting into the cheesecake. Put the pan in a larger one, such as a roasting pan, and pour boiling water in the gap between the two pans until the level is halfway up the springform pan. Bake according to the recipe.

Espresso Chocolate Fudge

The rich flavor of espresso is a perfect partner to the chocolate. For a homemade gift, place each piece of fudge in a paper or foil candy cup and arrange in a gift box lined with holiday paper.

Line an 8-inch baking dish with aluminum foil. Combine bittersweet chocolate, marshmallow crème, unsweetened chocolate, and vanilla in a medium bowl. Mix water and espresso powder in a heavy large saucepan until espresso powder dissolves. Add sugar, sweetened condensed milk, whipping cream, and unsalted butter and stir over medium heat until sugar dissolves, brushing down sides of pan occasionally with a wet pastry brush. Attach clip-on candy thermometer to side of pan. Increase heat to high and bring mixture to a boil. Reduce heat to medium and stir constantly but slowly with wooden spoon until candy thermometer registers 235°, about 12 minutes.

Immediately pour the mixture over the ingredients in the bowl (do not scrape pan). Stir the mixture vigorously with wooden spoon until all the chocolate melts and the fudge thickens slightly, about 3 minutes. Transfer the fudge mixture to the baking dish. Smooth the top of the fudge in pan with a rubber spatula. Refrigerate fudge uncovered until firm enough to cut, about 2 hours.

Using the aluminum foil as an aid, lift the fudge from pan. Trim the edges. Cut into 30 pieces. Melt the white chocolate in the top of a double boiler over simmering water. Using a fork, drizzle white chocolate decoratively over fudge. Refrigerate the fudge until the white chocolate sets, about 20 minutes. (Fudge can be prepared a week ahead. Store in airtight containers and refrigerate. Bring fudge to room temperature before serving.)

Carolyn Fredrick - Friend

Makes 30 pieces

6 ounces bittersweet (not unsweetened) or semisweet chocolate, chopped

¼ cup marshmallow crème

1 ounce unsweetened chocolate, chopped

1 teaspoon vanilla extract

½ cup water

2 tablespoons instant espresso powder

1 ½ cups sugar

¾ cup sweetened condensed milk

⅓ cup whipping cream

¼ cup (½ stick) unsalted butter

2 ounces high-quality white chocolate

Serves 8

5 ounces high-quality dark chocolate

6 tablespoons (¾ stick) butter

4 egg yolks

¾ cup unbleached flour

¾ cup sugar

4 egg whites, beaten until stiff peaks form

1 teaspoon rum

Dark Chocolate Frosting (below)

2 ounces dark chocolate

2 ounces butter (½ stick)

2 egg yolks

2 egg whites, beaten until stiff peaks form

Gâteau au Chocolat

The saying, "One can never be too rich or too thin," definitely applies to this cake! The secret lies in quality ingredients: unbleached flour, butter, and great chocolate. This makes a fairly small thin cake. Sometimes it's fun to double the recipe, bake two separate cakes, and add a layer of raspberry sauce between the layers. This recipe comes from a cookbook my grandmother gave me in France when I was 13. I've made it ever since.

Heat oven to 300°. Thoroughly grease a round cake pan. Break chocolate down in a saucepan and melt with butter on very low heat. Remove from heat and stir in egg yolks one at a time. Stir in flour and sugar, mix well. Add the beaten egg whites and rum. Spoon into pan and bake for 50 minutes. Frost immediately.

Dark Chocolate Frosting

Melt chocolate and butter over low heat. Once fully incorporated, remove from the stovetop and add egg yolks. Mix well. Gently fold in beaten egg whites. Spread over cake immediately. Frosting will harden when cool.

Veronique Poudrier - Product Development

Christmas cookies

Makes 2 dozen

5 ½ cups flour

2 teaspoons ginger

2 teaspoons cinnamon

1 teaspoon baking soda

1 teaspoon nutmeg

1 teaspoon cloves

½ teaspoon salt

1 cup shortening

1 cup sugar

1 cup molasses

2 eggs

GINGERBREAD COOKIES

Heat oven to 375°. Line cookie sheets with parchment. Sift together the flour, ginger, cinnamon, baking soda, nutmeg, cloves, and salt. Set aside.

In a saucepan, melt the shortening. Remove pan from heat. Beat in sugar and molasses. Beat in the eggs.

In a large mixing bowl, beat together the molasses mixture and about half of the flour mixture. Beat in the remaining flour. Divide dough in half, then cover each section with plastic wrap. Chill in the refrigerator for about 1 hour, or until easy to handle.

Roll out dough on a lightly floured surface to about ¼-inch thickness. Cut with cookie cutters. Arrange on a cookie sheet. Sprinkle with additional sugar, if desired. Bake for 6 to 8 minutes.

Remove from pan to wire rack. Frost when cool, if desired.

Kris Clifton - Friend

Hazelnut Gelato
with Warm Kahlúa Sauce

This dessert is "Shut-up good." You'll want all of your senses devoted to this marvelous dessert!

Finely grind hazelnuts in processor. Bring half-and-half to simmer in large saucepan. Whisk sugar and egg yolks in large bowl to blend. Gradually whisk hot half-and-half into sugar mixture; return to saucepan. Stir over medium heat until custard thickens slightly, about 3 minutes (do not let mixture boil). Pour through sieve into large bowl. Stir in hazelnuts and vanilla. Refrigerate custard until cold, about 4 hours. Transfer custard to ice cream maker and process according to manufacturer's instructions. Transfer custard to container; cover and freeze. Top with Warm Kahlúa Sauce.

Additional Serving Tip: Fill cream puffs with the gelato, drizzle Warm Kahlúa Sauce on top, and sprinkle with confectioners' sugar.

Serves 12

1 cup hazelnuts, toasted, husked

1 quart half-and-half

¾ cup sugar

3 large egg yolks

1 ½ teaspoons vanilla extract

Warm Kahlúa Sauce (below)

Warm Kahlúa Sauce

Bring half-and-half, sugar, and butter to simmer in a heavy medium saucepan, stirring until sugar dissolves. Remove from heat; add chocolate and whisk together until melted and smooth. Stir in Kahlúa and vanilla.

Note: This can be made 1 day ahead. Cool completely, cover, and refrigerate. Rewarm before serving.

Karen Mabee - Friend

Serves 12

1 cup half-and-half

¾ cup sugar

2 tablespoons (¼ stick) unsalted butter

1 ¼ pounds bittersweet or semi-sweet chocolate, chopped

¼ cup Kahlúa

1 teaspoon vanilla extract

key lime zingers

KEY LIME ZINGERS

Decorate these tangy cookies in green and white for a festive addition to your Christmas cookie tray.

Heat oven to 350°. In a large mixing bowl, beat butter with an electric mixer on medium to high speed for 30 seconds. Beat in sugar until light and fluffy. Add lime zest, lime juice, and vanilla. Beat in as much flour as you can. Using a wooden spoon, stir in any remaining four. Stir in nuts. Divide dough in half.

On a lightly floured surface, roll each half of dough about ¼ inch thick. Cut into desired shapes using cookie cutters. Place on ungreased cookie sheets. Bake for 8 to 10 minutes or until light brown around the edges. Cool on wire racks.

For frosting, beat cream cheese, confectioners' sugar, lime or lemon juice, and vanilla with an electric mixer on medium speed until smooth; tint as desired with food coloring. Frost cookies. Pipe designs with contrasting color of frosting, if desired.

Catherine Hill - Vera Bradley Foundation for Breast Cancer

Makes 6 dozen cookies

1 cup (2 sticks) butter

½ cup sugar

2 teaspoons key lime zest

¼ cup key lime juice (2 limes)

1 teaspoon vanilla extract

2 ¼ cups flour

¾ cup finely chopped Brazil nuts
  or hazelnuts

4 ounces cream cheese, softened

1 cup confectioners' sugar, sifted

1 tablespoon key lime or lemon juice

1 teaspoon vanilla extract

food coloring

Makes 2 dozen

2⅔ cups sweetened, flaked coconut

⅔ cup sugar

¼ cup flour

¼ teaspoon salt

4 egg whites, lightly whipped

1 teaspoon almond extract

1 cup chopped pecans

Macaroons

My mother, Mamie Clementine Dowdy, was the most wonderful cook I have ever known. Creativity had to abound because she had eight children. This is one of the after-school snacks we enjoyed.

Heat oven to 325°. Lightly grease your thickest cookie sheet. In a medium mixing bowl, combine coconut, sugar, flour, and salt. Stir in egg whites and almond extract. Stir in pecans. Drop by tablespoonfuls onto cookie sheet. Bake for 20 to 25 minutes or until golden brown.

Gloria Hansen - Retailer (Cupola House, Egg Harbor, Wisconsin)

Makes 4 dozen

1 cup (2 sticks) butter, softened

½ cup confectioners' sugar

2 teaspoons vanilla extract

2 cups flour

1 cup coarsely ground toasted pecans

1 ½ cups confectioners' sugar

⅛ teaspoon cinnamon

Mexican Wedding Cakes

These "cakes" are a holiday favorite and always pretty on a dessert tray.

Using an electric mixer, beat the butter in a large bowl until light and fluffy. Add the confectioners' sugar and vanilla; beat until well blended. Beat in flour, then pecans. Divide dough in half; form each half into a ball. Wrap separately in plastic; chill until cold, about 30 minutes.

Whisk the confectioners' sugar and cinnamon in a pie dish to blend. Set cinnamon sugar aside.

Heat oven to 350°. Line cookie sheets with parchment. Working with half of the chilled dough, roll dough by teaspoonfuls between palms into balls. Arrange the balls on baking sheet, spacing ½ inch apart. Bake the cookies until golden brown on the bottom and just pale golden on top, about 18 minutes. Cool cookies for 5 minutes on baking sheet.

Gently toss the warm cookies in cinnamon sugar to coat completely. Transfer coated cookies to rack and cool completely. Repeat procedure with remaining half of dough. (Cookies can be prepared 2 days ahead. Store in airtight containers at room temperature; reserve remaining cinnamon sugar.)

Sift remaining cinnamon sugar over cookies and serve.

Julie North - Human Resources

Mocha Logs

When you're after a cookie with a sophisticated flavor, try these tiny chocolate-dipped logs from 1969.

Heat oven to 375°. In a medium mixing bowl, beat the butter or margarine with an electric mixer on medium speed for 30 seconds. Add the sugar, espresso coffee powder, salt, and baking powder; continue beating. Add egg and vanilla. Gradually beat in the flour until blended.

Using a star plate in a cookie press, press dough in 3-inch-long strips onto an ungreased cookie sheets. Bake for 10 to 12 minutes. Transfer cookies to wire racks; let cool.

Dip ends of cookies in melted chocolate. Sprinkle finely chopped pecans over the chocolate.

Stefanie Chevillet - Friend

Makes 6 dozen

1 cup (2 sticks) butter or margarine

¾ cup sugar

4 teaspoons instant espresso coffee powder

½ teaspoon salt

¼ teaspoon baking powder

1 egg

1 teaspoon vanilla extract

2 ⅓ cups flour

8 ounces semisweet chocolate, melted and cooled

1 ½ cups finely chopped pecans

Sugar Cookies

The old-fashioned bakery style cookie.

Heat oven to 325°. Mix flour, baking soda, and salt together and set aside. Cream the shortening and sugar in a mixing bowl until light and fluffy. Beat in eggs. Add the flour mixture alternately with the buttermilk, beating constantly. Stir in vanilla. Add up to 1 additional cup of flour to make the desired rolling consistency, slightly sticky to the touch.

Roll out on a floured surface. Cut into desired shapes. Place on a nonstick cookie sheet. Bake for 7 to 10 minutes, or until golden brown.

Julie Clymer - Distribution

Makes 4 dozen

4 cups flour

2 teaspoons baking soda

1 teaspoon salt

1 cup shortening

2 cups sugar

2 eggs

1 cup buttermilk

2 teaspoons vanilla extract

WHITE CHOCOLATE AND PEPPERMINT COOKIE BRITTLE

Makes 2 dozen pieces

1 ½ cups flour

½ teaspoon baking soda

¼ teaspoon salt

¾ cup (1 ½ sticks) unsalted butter, melted, cooled slightly

½ cup sugar

⅓ cup golden brown sugar

1 teaspoon vanilla extract

10 ounces high-quality white chocolate, chopped into ⅓-inch pieces, divided

¾ cup coarsely crushed red-and-white-striped hard peppermint candies (about 6 ounces), divided

Heat oven to 350°. Line baking sheet with parchment. Whisk the flour, baking soda, and salt in a medium bowl. In a large bowl, whisk the melted butter, sugar, brown sugar, and vanilla until smooth. Stir in flour mixture until just blended. Stir in 1 cup chopped white chocolate and ½ cup crushed peppermint candy.

Transfer dough to prepared sheet. Press dough into 8x14-inch rectangle, about ⅜-inch thick. Bake for about 30 minutes or until top is firm and dark golden, slightly puffy. Cool on sheet 10 minutes. Transfer to rack; cool completely.

Stir remaining chocolate in top of double boiler over barely simmering water until melted and smooth. Using a small spoon, drizzle about half of melted chocolate in thin lines over cooled cookie. Sprinkle with remaining crushed peppermint candies. Drizzle remaining melted chocolate over the top. Let stand until white chocolate sets, about 1 hour. Break cookie into irregular 2- to 3-inch pieces. (Can be made 2 days ahead. Store in airtight container at room temperature.)

Beckie Hollenbeck - Merchandising

tree trimming party

CHAMPAGNE & FRUIT DRINKS

The perfect addition to any festive party is chilled champagne mixed with an assortment of chilled fruit juices. Here are a few tasty varieties:

MIMOSA: champagne and orange juice (Mix one part juice with two parts champagne)

POINSETTIA: champagne and cranberry juice (Mix one part juice with two parts champagne)

POMEGRANATE: champagne and one tablespoon of pomegranate juice

PRETTY WOMAN: champagne with a fresh strawberry. Watch it fizz . . .

Leigh Ann Dellinger & Jennifer Duell - Friends

Holiday Garnet Martini

Pictured on page 190.

Combine the cranberries, sugar, rosemary, and water in a medium size heavy saucepan over medium-low heat. Simmer uncovered, stirring occasionally, until cranberries pop and are very soft, about 30 minutes.

Pour cranberry mixture through a fine sieve into a bowl, gently stirring cranberries, but not pressing on them. Discard berries. Chill syrup, uncovered, until cold, about 3 hours.

Just before serving, stir together vodka and syrup in a pitcher. Serve over ice.

Michael Nelaborige - Friend

Serves 16

1 ½ pounds fresh cranberries

2 cups sugar

1 tablespoon finely chopped fresh rosemary

4 ½ cups water

1 (750-ml) bottle vodka

Hot Cranberry Pressé

You have to try this! It will fast become a winter favorite.

Boil cranberries and cinnamon in 12 cups water for 10 minutes. Cover and let steep for 15 minutes. Strain to remove solids. While liquid is hot, add lemon juice, orange juice, and sugar. Stir until sugar dissolves. Refrigerate any leftovers and heat as needed.

Nancy Ecclestone - Friend

Serves 16

1 (12-ounce) package fresh cranberries

2 sticks cinnamon

6 tablespoons lemon juice

1 ½ cups orange juice

1 to 2 cups of sugar (sweeten to taste)

Recipes by Category

Salads, continued

Side Dishes

Entrées

Desserts

Beverages

Recipes Alphabetically

Contributors

Sue Altum

Barbara Bradley Baekgaard

Becky Bennett

Julie Berghoff

Jim Berghoff

Sally Smith Berlin

Brigid Berry

Debra Bleeke

Lisa Boyd

Cher Bond

Lori Britton

Meghan Britton

Susan Britton

Diane Brown

Susie Bruce

Katie Burns

Leslie Byrne

Laura Byrne

Betheny Campbell

Mike & Maureen Catalogna

Stefanie Chevillet

Natalie Clark

Kris Clifton

Julie Clymer

Kim Colby

Sydney Colby

Melissa Cordial

Holly Crumpton

Mona Cunningham

Linda Cuzick

Dan's Tog Shop

LeighAnn Dellinger

Jennifer Duell

Nancy Ecclestone

Abby Ehinger

Aaron Feagler

Heidi Floyd

Adam Fox

Anne Frantz

Carolyn Fredrick

Peggy Gerardot

Susan Giles

Mary Ann Gray

Stacie Gray

Bill Gulledge

Nancy Graham

Joanie Byrne Hall

Jenny Hammons

Gloria Hansen

Betsy Lewis Harned

Peg Hattman

Lita Hegemier

Catherine Hill

Beckie Hollenbeck

Betty Howell

Kari Jefferis

Mary Jost

Sue Kelly

Sharon Keogh

Keith Kiess

Lyn Killoran

Vicki Kim

Jacque Klutz

Anne Korte

Margaret Krouse

Cheri Lantz

Terri Leonard

Renee Long

Phyllis Loy

Holly Lyon

Karen Mabee

Vi MacMurdo

Jenny Malone

Dana Manning

Yvonne Marson

Rosetta Mast

Joan Maxwell

Sophia McAlpin

Jenny Lynn McGee

Elizabeth Miller

Kate Miller

Patricia Miller

Michael Nelaborige

Joyce Neubauer

Pat Neulle

Jill Nichols

Julie North

Jean Oser

Tiffany Oser

Carol Overland

Patti Reedy Parker

Reba Peeples

Debbie Peterson

Gregory Phillpotts

Sally Pietzak

Patti Pine

Kathleen Piper

Nancy Pishney

Veronique Poudrier

Lila Pursley

Amy Byrne Ray

Kathy Reedy Ray

Joan Bradley Reedy

Glenna Reno

Lois Radke

Mark Sawyers

James Shimizu

Todd Shinabarger

Stephanie Scheele

Sharon Schomaker-Pruett

Margie Semonin

Lindsay Shumlas

Sue Stultz

Gail Tate

Tonya Tettenburg

Laura Vorderman

Holly Wagner

Mary Beth Wahl

Jeannine Wallace

Colleen Wegener

Donna Watson

Amber Whittington

Lois Whittington

Debbie Wilson

Judy Wintin

Rebecca Young

Wine Selection...
made simple

Choosing the right wine to go with different kinds of food can be intimidating, but it doesn't have to be. Most importantly, select a wine that you enjoy, rather than following some esoteric set of rules. Never mind the old adage about white wines going with fish or white meats and red wines going with red meats. In general, it's good to choose a lighter wine, whether red or white, for lighter foods or to enjoy alone, and choose heavier and more full-bodied wines for heartier and richer foods.

The following guide may help you in your choices. These are suggestions of types of wine, not brand names. Also, be aware that any guide like this is open to interpretation and question. If possible, find a local wine store with a good reputation where the staff can help you further define wines that suit your tastes and budget.

ALONE OR WITH APPETIZERS

Red — Beaujolais-Villages, Piedmont, Dolcetto, Pinot Noir, Côtes du Rhone, Sangiovese

White — Sauvignon Blanc, Chablis, Pouilly Fuisse, Riesling, Pinot Blanc, Champagne, Moscato Spumante, Prosecco

SEAFOOD

Red — Pinot Noir, Burgundy, Merlot

White — Vouvray, Pouilly Fuisse, Meursault, Graves, Fumé Blanc, Sancerre, Sauvignon Blanc, Montrachet, Pinot Grigio, Chablis, Chardonnay, Viognier

GAME BIRD/POULTRY

Red — Pinot Noir, Burgundy, Merlot

White — Sauvignon Blanc, Fumé Blanc, Pouilly Fuisse, Chardonnay, Riesling, Pinot Blanc, Gewürztraminer, Viognier

BEEF

Red — Cabernet Sauvignon, Bordeaux, Pinot Noir, Burgundy, Petite Syrah, Hermitage, Merlot, Shiraz, Rioja

LAMB

Red — Pinot Noir, Bordeaux, Burgundy, Cabernet Sauvignon, Merlot, Brunello

PORK

Red — Pinot Noir, Burgundy, Beaujolais, Sangiovese

White — Johannisberg Riesling, Kabinett, Australia Semillion/Traminer, Gewürztraminer

VEAL

Red — Burgundy, Pinot Noir

White — Sauvignon Blanc, Graves, Meursault, Riesling, Montrachet, Chablis, Pouilly Fumé, Chassagne-Montrachet, Bâtard-Montrachet, Corton-Charlemagne

GAME

Red — Petite Sirah, Hermitage, Barbaresco, Cabernet Sauvignon, Pinot Noir, Petite Syrah, Zinfandel, Burgundy, Merlot, Bordeaux, Brunello, Piedmont

SALADS

Red — Côtes du Rhone, Beaujolais, Sangiovese

White — Sancerre, Fumé Blanc, Sauvignon Blanc, Riesling, Graves

CHEESE

Red — Cabernet Sauvignon, Bordeaux, Burgundy, Shiraz, Port

White — Riesling, Kabinett, Chardonnay, Sauternes, Champagne

FRUITS

Red — Port

White — Riesling, Auslese, Trocken, Vouvray, Chenin Blanc, Gewürztraminer, demi-sec Champagne

DESSERTS

Red — Port

White — Barsac, Riesling, Sauternes, demi-sec Champagne, Moscato Spumante, Prosecco

Substitutions & Equivalents

Healthy Substitutions

498 mg. cholesterol 1 cup butter	=	2 sticks (1 cup) margarine *0 mg. cholesterol*
823 calories, 268 mg. cholesterol 1 cup heavy cream	=	1 cup evaporated skim milk *176 calories, 8 mg. cholesterol*
274 mg. cholesterol 1 medium whole egg	=	¼ cup egg substitute *0 mg. cholesterol*
250 calories 1 cup whole milk yogurt, plain	=	1 cup part skim milk yogurt, plain *125 to 145 calories*
416 calories 1 cup sour cream	=	1 cup puréed low-fat cottage cheese *208 calories*
8.4 grams saturated fat 1 ounce baking chocolate	=	3 tablespoons cocoa powder + 1 tablespoon polyunsaturated oil *2.8 grams saturated fat*

Herb and Spice Substitutions

Each herb and spice has its own distinct flavor and scent. These substitutions should only be used in emergencies, because they will affect the flavor of the finished recipe.

1 tablespoon fresh herbs	=	1 teaspoon dried herbs
1 teaspoon allspice	=	1 teaspoon equal parts cinnamon, nutmeg, and cloves
1 teaspoon basil	=	1 teaspoon oregano
1 teaspoon caraway	=	1 teaspoon anise
1 teaspoon cayenne	=	1 teaspoon chili peppers
1 teaspoon chervil	=	1 teaspoon parsley or tarragon
1 teaspoon fennel	=	1 teaspoon anise or tarragon
1 small garlic clove	=	⅛ teaspoon garlic powder or 1 teaspoon garlic salt (reduce salt by ½ teaspoon)
1 tablespoon fresh ginger	=	1 teaspoon powder or candied ginger with the sugar washed off
1 tablespoon mustard	=	1 teaspoon dried mustard
1 teaspoon nutmeg	=	1 teaspoon mace
1 small fresh onion	=	1 tablespoon dehydrated minced onion
1 medium fresh onion	=	1 tablespoon onion powder
1 teaspoon oregano	=	1 teaspoon marjoram
1 teaspoon sage	=	1 teaspoon thyme
dash cayenne or red pepper	=	few drops hot pepper sauce
fines herbs	=	equal parts of parsley, chives, tarragon, and chervil
bouquet garnie (herbs wrapped in cheese cloth) classic	=	2 sprigs parsley, ½ bay leaf, 1 sprig thyme or ⅛ teaspoon dried thyme
for lamb	=	rosemary, thyme, parsley, and celery
for veal	=	parsley, thyme, and lemon rind
for beef	=	basil, parsley, bay leaf, and clove

Measurement Equivalents

Dry Measures

1 cup	=	8 fluid ounces	=	16 tablespoons	=	48 teaspoons
¾ cup	=	6 fluid ounces	=	12 tablespoons	=	36 teaspoons
⅔ cup	=	5⅓ fluid ounces	=	10⅔ tablespoons	=	32 teaspoons
½ cup	=	4 fluid ounces	=	8 tablespoons	=	24 teaspoons
⅓ cup	=	2⅔ fluid ounces	=	5⅓ tablespoons	=	16 teaspoons
¼ cup	=	2 fluid ounces	=	4 tablespoons	=	12 teaspoons
⅛ cup	=	1 fluid ounce	=	2 tablespoons	=	6 teaspoons
		1 tablespoon	=	3 teaspoons		

Liquid Measures

1 gallon	=	4 quarts	=	8 pints	=	16 cups	=	128 fluid ounces
½ gallon	=	2 quarts	=	4 pints	=	8 cups	=	64 fluid ounces
¼ gallon	=	1 quart	=	2 pints	=	4 cups	=	32 fluid ounces
		½ quart	=	1 pint	=	2 cups	=	16 fluid ounces
		¼ quart	=	½ pint	=	1 cup	=	8 fluid ounces

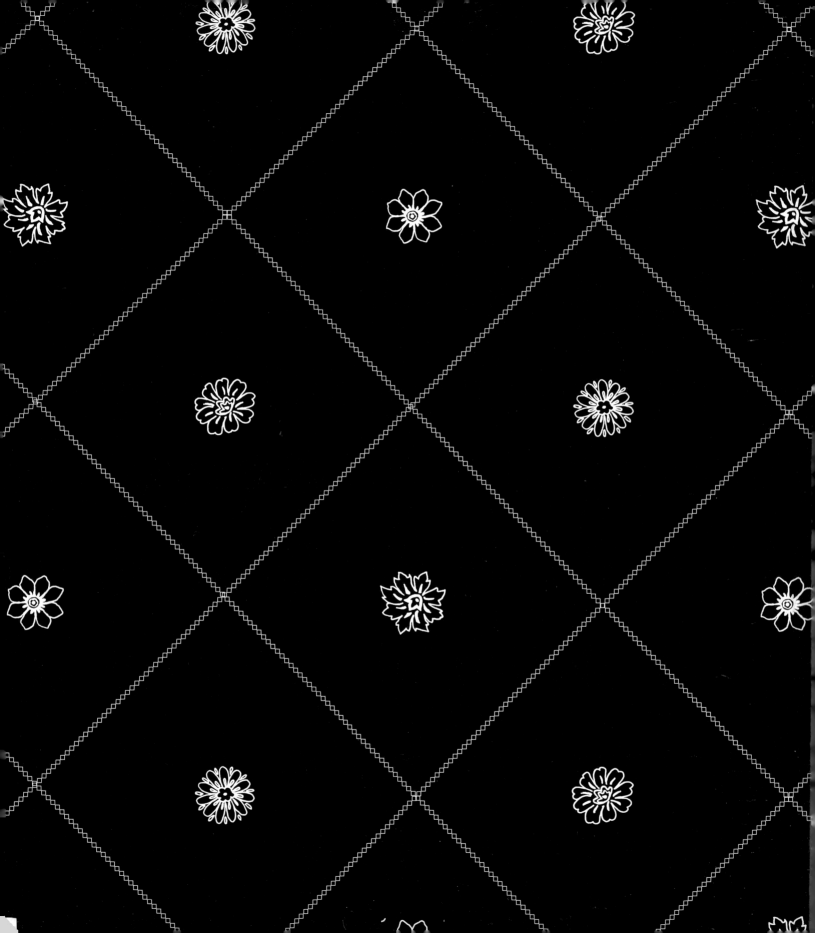